SCHELER'S PHENOMENOLOGY
OF
COMMUNITY

SCHELER'S PHENOMENOLOGY
OF
COMMUNITY

by

ERNEST W. RANLY, C.PP.S., Ph.D.

MARTINUS NIJHOFF / THE HAGUE / 1966

To my Dad (deceased)
to Mom
and to all the members of my family
this book
is
sincerely
dedicated

PREFACE

My own serious study of Max Scheler began in 1958 when I presented a Master's thesis to St. Louis University under the direction of Professor Vernon J. Bourke on Scheler's value-theory. Three years later when I returned to complete my doctorate work at St. Louis University I returned also to the study of Max Scheler. In the meantime, several more volumes of the *Gesammelte Werke* had appeared, several new translations of Scheler were published and the whole area of phenomenology began to be more favorably accepted by the American intellectual community. My doctoral dissertation was on Scheler's theory of community under the expert and careful direction of Professor James Collins. The bulk of the present work is a direct result of my work at St. Louis University.

I have never regretted the time and effort spent on the study of Scheler. He can be classified as nothing short of a genius, not only in the breadth of his interests but also in the vitality, unity and depth of his thought. Most students of Scheler criticize his lack of unity; I claim to find strong lines of inner consistency throughout his writings. In the second place, my study of Scheler has put me into contact with many of the most dominant intellectual influences of the day. Thus in Scheler one finds a distinct brand of phenomenology, an implicit existentialism, a theory of non-formal value-ethics, a philosophy of religion, a sociology of knowledge and a philosophical anthropology. In his theory of community there is a fresh investigation of the I-Thou, some fascinating studies on love, sympathy and shame and a classification of the forms of man's sociality by which he can both classify man's social structures and also make value judgments about actual historical societies.

Very recently (1965), Duquesne University Press has published *Max Scheler* by Manfred S. Frings. This is—in the words of its sub-title— "a concise introduction into the world of a great thinker." In ten chapters the author follows a topical outline, summarizing Scheler's teaching on the emotions, on values, man, God and so on. This is a good introduction, the only one available in English. Frings includes a selected bibliography of secondary works on Scheler; therefore, no such bibliography is included here. But I have included a bibliography on the primary works of Scheler. This should be an aid for future studies on Scheler.

At last, English studies on Scheler are being published. Several additional studies suggest themselves: on his philosophy of religion, on his epistemology of the emotions, on his value-ethics and on man as person. But also the time has come to expand Scheler's original seminal ideas into applied areas of ethics, sociology, religion and psychology, and applied specifically to the Anglo-American tradition of philosophizing. Finally, a last appeal: may we have an English translation of Scheler's *Der Formalismus* as accurate and as scholarly as we now have in the Macquarie-Robinson translation of Heidegger's *Sein und Zeit*. *Der Formalismus* of 1913 remains Scheler's major work. It is a personal manifesto of the spirit and method his phenomenological philosophy. It gave him, in outline and in principle, much of the content of his later philosophizing. It is an awkward, difficult book, but crucially important.

Some final notes of gratitude are in order. Among my fellow priests in the Society of the Precious Blood I am especially indebted to Fr. Edward Maziarz, my Dean at St. Joseph's College, and to Fr. Robert Lechner, editor of *Philosophy Today*, for their encouragement and inspiration, both by word and by example. To James Collins of St. Louis University I am indebted not only for his personal and patient directing of my research, but also for serving as a living ideal of a genuine Christian in scholarship. Within the "life-community" there is not only my own large family, but also there are the many other good friends (like the family down the street in St. Louis) and my colleagues who in many small but very significant ways made the publication of this book possible.

FR. ERNEST W. RANLY, C.PP.S.

St. Joseph's College
Rensselaer, Indiana
April, 1966

ACKNOWLEDGEMENTS

The author is grateful to The Messenger Press, Carthagena, Ohio, publisher of *Philosophy Today*, for permission to reprint the bulk of the article "Scheler on Man and Metaphysics" (Vol. 9, 211–221) which appears here in a slightly changed form in Chapter Two. For permission to print in this book from works still in copyright the author thanks the following publishers: the Friedrich Frommann Verlag, Stuttgart; the Francke Verlag, Bern; the G. Schulte-Bulmke Verlag, Frankfurt a. Main; the Nymphenburger Verlag, Munich; the S.C.M. Press, London; the Beacon Press, Boston; the Yale University Press, New Haven. In the case with each publisher, precise permission was asked covering all the individual texts cited in this study.

TABLE OF CONTENTS

LIST OF ABBREVIATIONS

A. The following abbreviations refer to the chief works of Scheler and the precise edition we are using in our own study.

1. *Ewigen. Vom Ewigen im Menschen.* Vierte durchgesehene Auflage. Herausgegeben von Maria Scheler. Bern: Francke, 1954. *Gesammelte Werke. (Ges. W.)*, Bd. 5.

2. *Formalismus. Der Formalismus in der Ethik und die materiale Wertethik.* Neuer Versuch der Grundlegung eines ethischen Personalismus. Vierte durchgesehene Auflage. Herausgegeben mit einem neuen Sachregister von Maria Scheler. Bern: Francke, 1954. *Ges. W.*, Bd. 2.

3. *Methode. Die transzendentale und die psychologische Methode.* Eine grundsätzliche Erörterung zur philosophischen Methodik. Leipzig: Dürr, 1900.

4. *Nachlass. Schriften aus dem Nachlass.* Band I. Zur Ethik und Erkenntnislehre. Zweite, durchgesehene und erweiterte Auflage. Mit einem Anhang. Herausgegeben von Maria Scheler. Bern: Francke, 1957. *Ges. W.*, Bd. 10.

5. *Soziologie. Schriften zur Soziologie und Weltanschauungslehre.* Zweite, durchgesehene Auflage. Mit Zusätzen und kleineren Veröffentlichungen aus der Zeit der Schriften. Herausgegeben mit einem Anhang von Maria Scheler. Bern: Francke, 1963. *Ges. W.*, Bd. 6.

6. *Stellung. Die Stellung des Menschen im Kosmos.* Fifth edition. München: Nymphenburger. 1947.

7. *Sympathie. Wesen und Formen der Sympathie.* Der "Phänomenoogie und Theorie der Sympathiegefühle" fünfte Auflage. Frankfurt/Main: G. Schulte-Bulmke, 1948.

8. *Umsturz. Vom Umsturz der Werte.* Abhandlungen und Aufsätze. Vierte durchgesehene Auflage. Herausgegeben von Maria Scheler. Bern: Francke, 1955. *Ges. W.*, Bd. 3.

9. *Weltanschauung. Philosophische Weltanschauung.* Dalp-Taschenbücher, Bd. 301. Bern: Francke, 1954. (Paperback.)

10. *Wissensformen. Die Wissensformen und die Gesellschaft.* Zweite, durchgesehene Auflage. Mit Zusätzen. Herausgegeben von Maria Scheler. Bern: Francke, 1960. *Ges. W.,* Bd. 8.

B. The following abbreviations refer to these five published English
translations of Scheler's works.

11. *Eternal. On the Eternal in Man.* Translated by Bernard Noble. London:
SCM Press, Ltd., 1960.
12. *Man's Place. Man's Place in Nature.* Translated, and with an intro-
duction, by Hans Meyerhoff. Boston: Beacon, 1961.
13. *Perspectives. Philosophical Perspectives.* Translated from the German by
Oscar A. Haac. Boston: Beacon, 1958.
14. *Ressentiment. Ressentiment.* Edited, with an Introduction by Lewis A.
Coser. Translated by William W. Holdheim. New York: The Free
Press of Glencoe, 1961.
15. *Sympathy. The Nature of Sympathy.* Translated from the German by
Peter Heath. With a general introduction to Max Scheler's work by
W. Stark. New Haven: Yale, 1954.

C. The following abbreviations refer to our own English titles of Scheler's works not translated into English. We are using the German
edition corresponding with the German abbreviation.

16. *Formalism. Formalismus.*
17. *Forms of Knowledge. Wissensformen.*
18. *Methods. Methode.*
19. *Overthrow. Umsturz.*
20. *Posthumous Writings. Nachlass.*
21. *Sociology. Soziologie.*

CHAPTER ONE

SCHELER ON PHILOSOPHY

To study some special theme in Max Scheler, it is necessary to locate that theme briefly within the totality of his thought. Scheler's life and works as a whole are still relatively unknown to English readers. There is need for an introduction to the life, works and personality of Scheler and to the method, spirit and content of his philosophy. Scheler's personality is an important factor in his total thought. Yet his thought must be studied carefully and critically in itself to discover where the real lines of inner unity and consistency lie. A comprehensive study of Scheler's phenomenology of community must attempt to understand this topic within the context of his total philosophy.

LIFE AND WRITINGS

Max Scheler was born at Munich on August 22, 1874. His father's family was Protestant. It traced back its lineage several centuries to the Bavarian town of Cobourg in Upper Franconia. His mother was Jewish, but also from a well established Franconian family. Religious influence upon the young Scheler was negligible.

Scheler took his humanities at the Luitpold and the Ludwig Gymnasia of Munich. He received instruction from a Catholic priest and was baptized at fourteen. This first religious orientation, however, seemed to lie dormant within the soul of Scheler: it had little direct influence upon the intellectual development of his formative years.

Entering the University of Munich in 1891, Scheler took up philosophy and the natural sciences. He continued these studies after his transfer to the University of Berlin. Here he took courses from William Dilthey, Carl Stumpf and Georg Simmel. Each of these men exerted a strong influence upon Scheler. Dilthey gave him a sense of the history of philosophy and introduced him to the philosophy of vitalism. Stumpf contributed the interest in and technique of descriptive psychology. Simmel was a combination of historian, sociologist and philosopher and introduced Scheler to the study of cultural forms.

After a short stay at Heidelberg, Scheler went to Jena where he received his doctorate in 1897 at the age of twenty-five. His courses included not only philosophy but also political economy and geography. Otto Liebmann was the Kantian scholar at Jena, noted for his insistence for a return "back to Kant!" and for his opposition to the neo-Kantians of the late nineteenth century. The most important influence upon Scheler's intellectual development during his student years was his major professor at Jena, Rudolf Eucken. Eucken introduced Scheler to Augustine and Pascal and to the philosophy of spirit. In all his early works, Scheler was very frank about his indebtedness to Eucken.

Scheler's Jena dissertation of 1897 was published two years later as *Studies towards the Determination of the Relations between Logical and Ethical Principles*.[1] Scheler's thesis was that logic and ethics are irreducible to each other, that there is a proper autonomy between the conditions of strict knowledge and the conditions of the moral life. Moral values are revealed in affective phenomena; these make up an independent, objective and permanent realm of moral reality for moral conscience. He attacked the rationalists and the Stoics who reduce the independent area of emotion and volition to purely rational principles. Scheler defended the objectivity and the independence of moral value by distinguishing between being and value, between the true and the good. In a recent critical study of Scheler, Dupuy has pointed out that this first work of Scheler's was not merely a commentary on the ideas of Eucken. Already here Scheler demonstrated the subtlety and the depth of his moral and psychological studies. He accepted certain fundamental principles and made a few basic distinctions which he was to maintain throughout his later works.[2]

In July of 1899 Scheler published a forty-page study entitled "Work and Ethics," the first of several essays on work. In the face of Marxism and the economic pressures of capitalism and mass production, Scheler defended the ethical and personal dimensions of work. Scheler remained at Jena through the years 1897 to 1907. He remained close

[1] No copy of this work is available. We are dependent upon the fine study of it made by Dupuy. M. Dupuy, *La philosophie de Max Scheler: Son évolution et son unité* (2 vls. Paris: Presses Universitaires, 1959), continuous pagination. Tome premier: *La critique de l'homme moderne et la philosophie théorique*; tome second: *De l'éthique à la dernière philosophie*. See Vol. 1, ch. I, "L'irréductibilité des principes éthique aux principes logique," 9–42.

[2] Dupuy, *op. cit.*, Vol. 1, 9. M. Frings, *Max Scheler* (Pittsburgh: Duquesne University Press, 1965), 223 pp. is the only full length study in English on the thought of Scheler. Frings follows a topical outline in his study which he labels "a concise introduction into the world of a great thinker." Frings' study is made from primary sources and is uniformly good. Unfortunately, it has appeared too recently to be of much positive aid for the present writer in this study on Scheler's theory of community.

to his master, Eucken, while conducting his own courses in philosophy.

Also in 1899 Scheler submitted his *Habilitationsschrift* to the University of Jena for advancement to the rank of *Privatdozent*. This work, openly indebted to Eucken, was entitled *Transcendental and Psychological Methods*. After a short historical survey of modern philosophical methods, Scheler took up first the exposition and critique of Kant's transcendental method, and then the exposition and critique of contemporary methods in psychology. Scheler's criticism of Kant continued for the next two decades. His own critical reaction to psychologism paralleled very closely the intellectual development of Edmund Husserl.[1] Scheler concluded this study on method by listing twelve concluding theses. The proper method of philosophy he called the "noological method," a term borrowed from Eucken but which Scheler felt was expendable. "Philosophy is the study of spirit [*die Lehre vom Geiste*]." The noological method was to bring the higher rationalism of Kant into a living philosophy of spirit (*die geistliche Lebensform*) and to combine this with the positivistic-psychological approach to human experience and culture (*die Arbeitswelt*). The former is irreducible to the latter. Here is a theme which returned at the end of Scheler's life. Scheler also declared that the philosophical method cannot presume to grant a privileged position to any single datum, as if anything were valid before investigation. In this principle Scheler was already in possession of a basic habit of thought fundamental to phenomenology.

In 1901 Scheler met Husserl for the first time at Halle. Hans Vaihinger had called together the collaborators of *Kantstudien*. Scheler himself described the occasion:

A philosophical discussion ensued regarding the concepts of intuition (*Anschauung*) and perception. The writer, dissatisfied with Kantian philosophy, to which he had been close until then (he had for this reason just withdrawn from the printer a half completed work on logic), had come to the conviction that what was given to our intuition was originally much richer in content than what could be accounted for by the sensuous elements, by their derivatives, and by their logical patterns of unification. When he expressed this opinion to Husserl and remarked that this insight seemed to him a new and fruitful principle for the development of theoretical philosophy, Husserl pointed out at once that in a new book on logic, to appear presently [i.e., the *Logische Untersuchungen*, volume II], he had worked out an analogous enlargement

---

[1] Edmund Husserl (born April 8, 1859) took early studies in mathematics, science and philosophy. While at the University of Halle he wrote the *Philosophy of Arithmetic* (1891), which gave a psychological explanation for mathematics. Over the next ten years Husserl continued his study of mathematics and logic, but he underwent an intellectual conversion in rejecting psychology as the master science of human disciplines. Husserl gave public expression of his change of kind in the publication of the two volumes of *Logical Investigations* in 1900–01. Volume One contains Husserl's famous polemic against psychologism. In the same year he assumed a teaching position at the University of Göttingen.

of the concept of intuition (*kategoriale Anschauung*). The intellectual bond between Husserl and the writer, which has become so extraordinarily fruitful for him, dates back to this moment.[1]

There was a simultaneous but independent discovery by Scheler and Husserl of some of the most basic starting points of phenomenology. Scheler continued teaching at Jena until 1907 when he moved back to his native city and taught at the University of Munich for three years. At Munich, since 1894, Theodor Lipps had been teaching a brand of descriptive psychology. His close circle of students reacted sharply to Husserl's attack against Lipps and all forms of psychologism in the *Logical Investigations* of 1901. In 1903 one of these students (Johannes Daubert) bicycled to Göttingen, had a twelve-hour discussion with Husserl, and returned to Munich, afire with enthusiasm for phenomenology. The following year Husserl himself addressed the Munich Circle. Lipps saw his group turn away from him to phenomenology. When Scheler joined the Munich Circle in 1907 it already included Daubert, Alexander Pfänder, Adolph Reinach, Theodor Conrad, Moritz Geiger, Aloys Fischer and August Gallinger. (A little later Dietrich von Hildebrand joined the Circle.) Scheler learned much from the frequent, enthusiastic meetings of the Munich Circle. He contributed more than his share to the group's interests in problems of value, ethics and aesthetics. Meanwhile, a similar group formed around Husserl at Göttingen. This latter group followed the lead of their teacher and concentrated more on logical, mathematical and epistemological problems.[2]

In 1910 Scheler lost his position at the University of Munich.[3] For

---

[1] From P. Witkop, ed., *Deutsches Leben der Gegenwart* (Berlin: Wegweiser, 1922), 197–98. As quoted (and translated) by H. Spiegelberg, *The Phenomenological Movement: A Historical Introduction* (2 vols. The Hague: Martinus Nijhoff, 1960), 229. Cf., Dupuy, *op. cit.*, Vol. I, 101–102; also Q. Lauer, S.J., "The Phenomenological Ethics of Max Scheler," *International Philosophical Quarterly*, 1 (1961), 277. This essay of Scheler's on contemporary German philosophy was written in 1922 (to appear in Band 7 of the *Gesammelte Werke*). It is to be noted, then, that Scheler is writing from personal memory about an event over twenty years in the past. One wonders whether Scheler himself in 1901 had already thought out the detailed implications of his views on intuition. At the time, Husserl had more to teach Scheler than *vice versa*. Also, it seems that Scheler's anti-Kantianism did not come to full term until after 1904, for in that year he wrote a centennial piece favorable to Kant; cf. Dupuy, *op. cit.*, Vol. 1, 102, n. 2.

[2] A short colorful history of these early phenomenological groups is given by Spiegelberg, *op. cit.*, 168–73. He also has published a most interesting photograph of the Göttingen Circle of 1912 (opposite p. 170), as well as individual photographs of Pfänder, Daubert, Reinach and Geiger (opposite p. 173).

[3] Dupuy states: "En 1910, des circonstances personnelles contraignirent Scheler à quitter l'enseignement," *op. cit.*, Vol. 2, 726. Years before, Scheler had entered a civil marriage with a divorcée. Upon his return to Munich he managed to free himself from this bond, but not without much personal loss and suffering. See: J. Oesterreicher, "Max Scheler, Critic of

the next nine years he had no academic position. As a *Privatgelehrter* Scheler lived in very difficult material circumstances, but this was a period of most productive intellectual activity.[1] The first few years he spent at Göttingen near Husserl and the Göttingen Circle. Later he lived at Berlin with the close association of Walter Rathenau and Werner Sombart.

Scheler's lectures at Jena from 1901 to 1906 and at Munich from 1907 to 1910 continued his interests in ethical questions. At Göttingen in 1910–11 and again in 1911 Scheler gave two formal series of lectures to the Circle of Husserl's students entitled simply "Problems of Ethics." In the meantime he began a number of independent phenomenological investigations on death, shame, freedom, the idea of God and epistemology.[2] These works remained unpublished until 1933 but much of their significance is lost if they are not studied in the context of Scheler's developing thought. In 1911 Scheler published the short essay "On Self-Delusions." In 1912 he published a longer essay, "On *Ressentiment* and the Moral Value-Judgment." Because of these two studies, several scholars gave Scheler the title: Critic of Modern Man. The first edition of his work on sympathy also appeared in 1913 under the title: *Towards the Phenomenology and Theory of the Feeling of Sympathy and on Love and Hatred.*

At this time Scheler and several other phenomenologists worked together with Husserl to co-edit and co-found the *Jahrbuch für Philosophie und phänomenologische Forschung*. The purpose of the new journal was to publish the various phenomenological investigations undertaken by Husserl's students. The first volume of the *Jahrbuch* appeared in 1913. Part Two of this first issue consisted of the first part of Scheler's major work, *Formalism in Ethics and Material Value-Ethics*.[3] Scheler had Part

Modern Man," *Walls Are Crumbling: Seven Jewish Philosophers Discover Christ.* (New York: The Devin-Adair Company, 1953), 141–42.

[1] See Posselt (Sister Teresia de Spiritu Sancto, O.D.C.), *Edith Stein* (New York: Sheed and Ward, 1951), 43–46, for the reactions of the young Edith Stein to the genius of Scheler during his Göttingen years. In charming frankness, Edith Stein described Scheler as a genius, but who "in practical matters was as helpless as a child."

[2] These works remained in manuscript form and were published only posthumously in one volume in 1933. The second enlarged edition is Band 10 of the *Gesammelte Werke.* M. Scheler, *Schriften aus dem Nachlass: Band I. Zur Ethik und Erkenntnislehre.* (Bern: Francke, 1957). For complete details on this and all the works of Scheler cf. the Bibliography.

[3] The translation of this title remains disputed. Stark translates the first half as: "The Formalistic Principle in Ethics." (W. Stark, "Editor's Introduction." M. Scheler, *The Nature of Sympathy* [New Haven: Yale University Press, 1954.], pp. xiv–xvi.) Today, however, the Kantian meaning of "formalism" is generally accepted. The translation of the first half of Scheler's work seems most appropriate and intelligible with "Formalism in Ethics." The second half creates greater difficulty. Stark continues: "*Die materiale Wertethik* is translated here as 'the non-formal ethic of value' in order to bring out the contrast, intended by

Two prepared by 1914 but World War I prevented its publication until 1916 when it appeared as the second volume of the *Jahrbuch*. In the same year a special edition reprinted both parts of *Formalism* into a single volume.

Scheler threw himself into the war effort with characteristic enthusiasm. He served in the German Foreign Office from 1917 to 1918, accepting missions to Geneva and to The Hague. In 1915 Scheler published *The Spirit of War and the German War*, a piece of German war propaganda which also investigated the phenomenon of the war experience. It is unfair to consider this work as being nothing more than German propaganda. *War and Reconstruction* of 1916 contains several studies of lasting merit. It is here that Scheler gives expression to the idea of the collective consciousness not only of a single nation, but of the whole world as being at war. Scheler proceeded to instruct the German national consciousness with two further works: *The Causes of the Hatred for Germany* (1917) and *Two German Diseases* (1919).

In 1916 Dom Anselm Manser, O.S.B., Abbot of the Benedictine Abbey of Beuron, received Scheler back into the Catholic Church. This second conversion at the age of forty-two had direct and immediate influence upon Scheler's intellectual and literary activity of the next six years. This period of Scheler's life is often called the "Catholic Period." Scheler's writings of the later war years strongly reflect his newly rediscovered Catholic faith. The publication of *On the Eternal in Man* in 1921 was Scheler's major work in the philosophy of religion. This work was the fruit and the climax of his Catholic years.

In 1919 Scheler accepted the Chair of Philosophy and Sociology at

Scheler, to the 'formal principle' of Kant. It is, of course, totally inadmissible and absolutely misleading to speak of Scheler's 'Ethics of Material Values'..." *Ibid.*, n. 1. Collins translates this part as "the Ethics of Intrinsic Value" (J. Collins, "The Moral Philosophy of Max Scheler," *Encyclopedia of Morals* [New York: Philosophical Library, 1956], 518.) Schutz translates: "the Material Ethics of Value." (A. Schutz, "Max Scheler's Epistemology and Ethics," *The Review of Metaphysics*, 11 [1957–58], 486.) Noble speaks of "the ethics of supra-formal values." (M. Scheler, *On the Eternal in Man* [London: SCM Press, Ltd., 1960], 458 and n. 2; 279, n. 1. Meyerhoff translates this as "an Ethics of Objective Values." (H. Meyerhoff, "Translator's Introduction," M. Scheler, *Man's Place in Nature* [Boston: Beacon Press, 1961], P. xvi.) In our Master's thesis of 1958 we defended the translation "Material Value-Ethics." (E. Ranly, C.PP.S., *Max Scheler: Theory of Value-Ethics: An Introduction*. [St. Louis: St. Louis University, 1958], 20–22.) We still prefer this rendition. Obviously, it is the most direct translation. It needs explanation, but so do all its circumlocutions. The Kantian-Humean epistemological context of the meaning of form and matter must be understood. In rejecting the formalistic ethics of Kant, Scheler devised a theory by which ethical values are perceived in directly intuiting the immediately given "matter" of experience. His own title remains ambiguous to this extent. Does Scheler mean "the material ethics of value" or "The ethics of material value"? We are willing to retain this original ambiguity with the translation: "Material Value-Ethics."

the University of Cologne and the position of Director of the Institute of Social Studies. He remained at Cologne until 1928. Over the next few years, academic matters did not prevent Scheler from publishing *Eternal*, his major work on religion, several smaller studies, and re-editing his work on sympathy and his early essays in sociology. He continued to develop his theory on the sociology of knowledge. At the same time Scheler began to give public evidence of a rather radical shift in metaphysics and a movement away from traditional theism to an evolutionary anthropological pantheism. This led to a public repudiation of his Catholic faith.[1] *Forms of Knowledge and Society* in 1926 represents Scheler's final detailed statement in sociology. His long promised work on anthropology was never fully completed. *The Place of Man in Nature* appeared in 1927, a small book, highly condensed, but it is Scheler's last exposition of his philosophical anthropology and his later views on the incomplete, evolving deity. In the work *Philosophical Weltanschauung* published a year after his death there are gathered together five of Scheler's last short works.

In the spring of 1928 Max Scheler accepted a position at the University of Frankfort on the Main. He died suddenly of a coronary thrombosis on May 19, 1928, at the age of fifty-four at Cologne.

A mere sketch of Scheler's life shows that he was no traditional academic philosopher. His interests were as broad as the horizons. All that he did he did enthusiastically, enspirited almost with a Platonic *daimon*. Scheler's life, his philosophy and his dynamic influence cannot be divorced from his personality. His philosophical interests tended to shift with his personal involvements. His close friends and associates universally attest to the magnetism of his person and of his discourses.[2] To read Scheler today is to catch some spark of the flame that burned in his heart and head.

---

[1] Scheler gave evidence of a shift in thought already at the end of 1922. This first became explicit in his preface to *Soziologie*; cf. Dupuy, *op. cit.*, Vol. 2, 728. Scheler's personal life continued to be troubled with sudden, abrupt changes. His marriage with Maria Furtwängler (daughter of Professor Adolph Furtwängler of Munich, archaeologist and art collector, and a niece of Wilhelm Furtwängler, the noted German conductor) was solemnly blessed by the Church. However, several years later, Scheler was annoyed when the Church refused to annul the marriage to allow him to marry a former student. He repudiated the Catholic legislation on marriage and married Maria, the present editor of the *Gesammelte Werke*.

[2] For special studies on Scheler's personality see Dupuy, *op. cit.*, note II, "La personnalité de Scheler," Vol. 2, 729–39; H. Lützler, *Der Philosoph Max Scheler: Eine Einführung*. (Bonn: H. Bouvier u. Co., 1947); D. von Hildebrand, "Max Scheler als Persönlichkeit," *Hochland*, 26 (1928–29), 232–65. (Reprinted in his *Zeitliches im Lichte des Ewigen*. [Regensburg: Josepf Habbel, 1932]; Oesterreicher, *op. cit.* General studies on Scheler almost to a fault tend to concentrate upon character-description rather than upon a critical analysis of his writings.

In view of the towering strength of Scheler's personality, it is difficult to give a fair assessment of his philosophy. That personality blinds both his friends and his enemies to the intrinsic merits of his thought. Perhaps now, a generation removed from Scheler, with the definitive edition of his collected works in the process of publication, it will be possible to begin anew the controlled critical study of Scheler's thought.

MEANING AND METHOD OF PHILOSOPHY

To over-emphasize the restlessness and the instability of Scheler's character is to suggest that the developments and changes in his thought are little more than reflections of his basic instability of character.[1] In Husserl's terms, this would be a case of using "psychologism" to analyze the thought of a man. A genuine critical study of Scheler must examine his thought carefully with an awareness of the importance of chronology, to discover the inner structure and content of that thought. Changes in thought would then be seen to be inner organic developments, rather than mere whims of personality. Criticism will then be relevant to the intrinsic argument of the man's thought.

To find a basic unity in Scheler's thought it seems most appropriate to discuss first his conception of philosophy itself: its meaning, its spirit, its method, its content. In his *Habilitationsschrift* of 1897, Scheler was critical of both the transcendental and the psychological method in philosophy. His conclusion at that time was to use the "noological method" of Eucken in order to combine in philosophy the irreducible function of spirit with the empirical elements of everyday experience. The nature of Scheler's reflective mind forced him to place all data

---

[1] Much discussion has arisen over the reasons for and the significance of Scheler's transition from Catholicism to pantheism. For a brief discussion, see Ranly, *op. cit.*, 6–10. Von Hildebrand and Oesterreicher try to explain Scheler's defection from the Faith (and from theism) by reason of personality faults that made him rush off heedlessly into contrary directions. Von Hildebrand personally has never abandoned his point of view that subjectively and objectively Scheler was always a Catholic: it was a sense of irrational pride that forced Scheler to defend theoretically his opposition to the Church. Häcker in "Geist and Leben: Zum Problem Max Scheler," *Hochland*, 23 (1926), states that Scheler never was a Catholic, subjectively or objectively. Collins in "Scheler's Transition from Catholicism to Pantheism," *Philosophical Studies in Honor of the Very Reverend Ignatius Smith, O.P.* (Westminster, Maryland: The Newman Press, 1952), 179–202; reprinted in J. Collins, *Three Paths in Philosophy* (Chicago: H. Regnery, 1962), "Roots of Scheler's Evolutionary Pantheism," 106–131, reviews some of the past discussion and takes a more realistic and critical point of view on the "problem of Max Scheler." Collins traces Scheler's line of reasoning to its methodological basis. He discovers a large amount of common doctrine in the early and later Scheler, so that Scheler's evolution to anthropological pantheism is seen to rest upon some general methodological and metaphysical bases in Scheler's whole essentialistic approach to philosophy.

under investigation. By 1901, and surely during his Munich years of 1901 to 1910, Scheler was convinced of the need to subject the original data of intuition to direct and thorough scrutiny. During these years he was thoroughly taken up with the fresh new method of phenomenology, but for ten years he published nothing.

In 1911 there appeared the essay "On Self-Delusions." This was the first of Scheler's public studies in phenomenology. He expressed his deep indebtedness to the work of Husserl, while making his own preliminary investigations into many areas of human psychology.[1] The following year Scheler published a more concentrated phenomenological study on the emotion of *ressentiment*. In the Prefatory Remarks, Scheler briefly distinguished his own method of "analytic and descriptive psychology" from the method of scientific psychology. The latter artificially breaks up man's experiences into simple elements in an effort to give a causal explanation of psychic facts. His own method tried to *understand* (*Verstehen*) the very meaning of man's experience in the unified totality of a "phenomenologically simple" experience. Thus, the purpose of this essay was "to examine *ressentiment* as one such unity of experience and action."[2] His studies on sympathy, love and hatred were further concrete phenomenological studies of human emotions. The work on sympathy in 1912–13 was "to provide an example of how to conduct investigations into the phenomena of the emotional life."[3] Scheler had completed several other studies during this time, but these remained unpublished until after his death.

Scheler's most important work was his major work on ethics, *Formalism*. This was both a "Summa" of his thought and a concrete application of method. It was a huge, sprawling book, repetitious at times, and suggestive of many possible developments. In the Foreword to the Third Edition in 1926, Scheler could justifiably declare that the basic principles and insights of *Formalism* need not be changed to account for

[1] *Umsturz*, 246–47. Scheler noted a change of mind in Husserl from the *Logical Investigations* of 1900 to the *Logos* essay of 1910 concerning philosophy as a strict science. Scheler briefly criticized Husserl and suggests that a phenomenology of essences is just as successful in psychology and the sciences as when Husserl employs it in logic and mathematics.

[2] *Ressentiment*, 39. (A direct reference to the English work means that we are quoting literally the English text from the text as cited.) "Als eine solche Erlebnis- und Wirkungseinheit sei im folgenden das *Ressentiment* einer Untersuchung unterzogen." *Umsturz*, 36. In a note, Scheler refers to Karl Jasper's distinctions between causal connections (*Kausal, zusammenhänge*) and the understandable context in mental life (*Verständniszusammenhänge*). However, the discussion here is in the tradition of Husserl's anti-psychologism of the *Logical Investigations* of 1900, where those same distinctions are analyzed at some length.

[3] *Sympathy*, p. 1. "Gleichzeitig möchte die kleine Schrift ein Beispiel dafür sein, auf welche Weise Untersuchungen über die Phänomene des Gemütslebens zu führen sind." *Sympathie*, XVII.

his own intellectual development from theism to evolutionary pantheism. It would be misleading to classify Scheler's total thought as comprising a "system." Yet there was much about the spirit and structure of *Formalism* and its continued role in Scheler's thought that is comparable to Kant's first *Critique*.

One characteristic feature of *Formalism* was its attack on the presuppositions of Kant's formal system of ethics. Scheler exposed Kant's ethics to the same mode of criticism that Husserl had employed against psychologism: an exposition and a detailed refutation of its unexpressed presuppositions. In 1928 Scheler declared:

> Whoever strives for a *Weltanschauung* that is philosophically grounded must dare to stand on his *own* reason. He must tentatively doubt all previously accepted opinions and dare to acknowledge nothing that is not clearly seen and established by himself personally.[1]

Husserl had made these conditions the program for a fully rigorous and strictly scientific philosophy.[2] Scheler's aim was to employ the same rigorous method in the construction of a strictly scientific phenomenology of ethics. He repeatedly asserted that the primary purpose of *Formalism* was not to refute Kant but to investigate phenomenologically the given data of the immediate moral experience.

Scheler spoke of the "phenomenological experience" as an immediate phenomenological intuition into the essence or form of the direct objective content of an experience. This *content* or *form* is essence or nature, *Was, Wesen* or *Wesenheit*. This pure essence as directly intuited (by a *Wesensschau*) is a pure *Phänomen*. It is an essence that is self-given. As such, it is neither individual nor universal. For example, to examine phenomenologically the "essence" of redness we do not combine many red things into a common experience, we do not investigate this individual red *thing*, but we try to intuit directly the essence of pure "redness" by actually catching the objective content of redness within a "red-experiencing" experience. Such an experiencing act (*Tat*) contacts the object of the experience, a given, a datum (*Sache*). Necessarily, the given is intuited only within the act so that together they form a phenomenological fact (*Tatsache*). Pure essences are further seen to

---

[1] (Translation our own.) "Wer aber eine philosophisch begründete Weltanschauung anstrebt, muss es wagen, sich auf seine *eigene* Vernunft zu stellen. Er muss alle hergebrachten Meinungen versuchsweise bezweifeln und darf nichts anerkennen, was ihm nicht persönlich *einsichtig* und begründbar ist." *Weltanschauung*, 5. Cf. M. Scheler, *Philosophical Perspectives* (Boston: Beacon Press, 1958), 1.

[2] E. Husserl, "Philosophie als strenge Wissenschaft," translated by Q. Lauer, S.J., "Philosophy as a Strict Science," *Cross Currents*, 6 (1950), 227–46, 325–44.

have set relationships to other essences (*Wesenszusammenhänge*). For example, "redness" must be further qualified by some spatial dimension, with some shape or figure. Such combinations of given data (*Sachverhalte*) are not constructed by the mind, nor are they reasoned to inductively or deductively. They are simply discovered and acknowledged as being related in a particular manner. It is in this sense that phenomenology seeks to unveil the actual pre-given conditions of things and thus to discover the *a priori* order and laws given within the pure essences themselves.[1] Husserl had begun such a study of pure logic; Scheler's prime interest was to investigate the *a priori* essences, the relationships and the order of emotional values.

Within *Eternal*, published in 1921, Scheler included a forty-page essay entitled "On the Nature of Philosophy." He had written this study in 1916–17. Its sub-title was: "The Moral Condition of Philosophical Knowledge." On the one hand, Scheler disagreed with Husserl's use of the term *science* as applied to philosophy. But the major part of this study was Scheler's own statement on philosophy as being a total engagement of the person in the act of philosophizing and the moral conditions for that act.

Scheler stated again here the requirement that philosophy be free from all presuppositions, that it be autonomous. "Philosophy must first constitute *itself* by asking what its own nature may be."[2] Philosophy "seeks and finds its essence and principle exclusively *through itself*, in itself and in its constitution."[3] He turned to historical instances of philosophers actually philosophizing to discover what the essence (*Wesen*) of philosophy may be. In other words, the act of philosophizing must itself be phenomenologically investigated to discover and define the essence of philosophy. The peculiar sphere of reality accessible only through a special intellectual attitude (*Geisteshaltung*) is a world all its own, constituted

---

[1] For an explicit discussion by Scheler on the method of phenomenology as understood and employed by him, see *Formalismus*, 68–72. All of chapter II, "Formalismus and Apriorismus," 66–130, is a fine exposition of Scheler's early phenomenology. It is difficult to translate Scheler's phenomenological meaning of *Wesen* into English. However, *Essence* is to be preferred to *nature*. *Nature* suggests too positively the extramental reality of a thing. *Essence*, too, must be carefully restricted to its phenomenological meaning. However, no consistent tradition is being formed in English phenomenology and the translations as well as original discussions use the terms interchangeably. (E.g. we have the published English translation of *The Nature of Sympathy* for the *Wesen und Formen der Sympathie*.) In this present study, *Wesen* is always translated as *essence*, unless the English construction demands otherwise.

[2] *Eternal*, 69. "Die Philosophie ... sich durch die Frage nach ihrem Wesen gleichsam *selbst* erst zu konstituieren hat...." *Ewigen*, 63.

[3] *Eternal*, 70, "Ihr Wesen und ihre Gesetzlichkeit ausschliesslich *durch sich selbst* und in sich selbst und ihrem Bestande suchende und findende." *Ewigen*, 64.

in the very intuiting of it—the philosophical *Weltanschauung*.[1] The
act of philosophizing is the very constituting of philosophy itself.

The act of philosophizing is an integral act of the very core of the
human person. It is defined as: "the love-determined act of participation by the core of a finite human person towards the essential factors
of all possible things."[2] For Scheler there is an ontological and temporal
moment of *love*, of vitalistic impulse, prior to the act of knowledge. One
can know only what he loves. Philosophy, as a very special type of
activity by the human person, seeks participation in no lower level of
being. Its impulse is towards the absolute being of Primary Essence
(*eine Teilnahme am Sein des Urwesens*). But at the same time, philosophy is
always and essentially a *cognitive* activity. It seeks participation in being
through knowledge. There is an ambiguity here between "loving participation in being" and "essential knowledge" which divides Scheler's
meaning of philosophy as well as his theory of being.

There are two fundamental moral conditions for philosophy. The first
demands a sense of asceticism in order to deny the absolute reality of the
lower levels of being. The basic intellectual attitude of the philosopher
cannot be satisfied with the natural world nor with the mere probable
opinions of the scientists (Plato's *doxa*); philosophy seeks the true knowledge of *episteme*. Only in this way can philosophy retain its autonomy
and its ancient title of Queen of the Sciences. The second moral condition
for philosophy is the vital commitment of the whole person to participation
with being. This is a moral elevation, an "upsurge" (*Aufschwung*), of the
whole person adhering faithfully to the primary love-act by the person
towards being. Any practical orientation of knowledge can only *follow*
this perfectly free autonomous investigation of being and values. To
reverse the procedure is a primary instance of the subversion of values.
In the essay of 1916–17, Scheler discussed theoretically the various
possible personal commitments of Plato, Buddha, Fichte and Bergson
to different conceptions of the Primary Being. But at this time, Scheler's
own personal commitment to Christianity helped to direct and restrain
his own self-dedication in pursuit of Being. However, his program for
philosophy was set. He continued to throw himself enthusiastically into
the study of values (even the values of war), the study of the basic
biological life-impulse and the study of man. According to his own

---

[1] Scheler's terms here are: *geistliche Grundhaltung, die philosophische Geisteshaltung* and *philoso-phische Weltanschauung*.

[2] (Our own translation.) "Liebesbestimmter Aktus der Teilnahme des Kernes einer end-lichen Menschperson am Wesenhaften aller möglichen Dinge." *Ewigen*, 68. Cf. *Eternal*, 74.

program, Scheler could only abandon himself to the essential realities of things as he was to discover them for himself.[1] Scheler emphasized the moral conditions for philosophy, since he understood philosophy to be an intense personal act of the concrete whole of the human spirit. Its essentially cognitive activity is possible only upon the realization of many non-cognitive factors. He listed three basic moral acts necessary for philosophizing: 1) love of the whole spiritual person for absolute value and being; 2) the humbling of the natural self; 3) a mastery over self to achieve true philosophical insights into self-evident essences.[2] Philosophy must rise above the natural world outlook of the common man (*natürliche Weltanschauung*) and above the positivistic sciences of the day (*wissenschaftliche Weltauffassung*) to achieve the moral-intellectual attitude of the philosopher.

The first self-evident insight for the phenomenological philosopher is that "there is something" or, negatively, "there is not nothing." The insight here is into a relative, contingent entity. However, following upon the phenomenological suspension of reality ("bracketing"), it is unclear if this is an insight into *real* being or merely into *ideal* (mental) being. Scheler moved rather recklessly into a second immediate self-evident insight, that "absolute entity which simply *is* must be the ground for all relative entity." Finally, a third self-evident insight is that there is a distinction between the qualitative *quid est*, the essence of a thing, and its existence.[3]

These insights may have been rather arbitrarily hit upon by Scheler, but they give him the fundamentals for a purely rational conception of metaphysics. In his later essay on "The Problems of Religion" Scheler strongly maintained that the intentional object of metaphysics was a purely theoretical notion. Its origin, its essence and its meaningful significance for man are totally independent from a *religious* knowledge of God. "The goal of religion is not rational knowledge of the basis of the world but the *salvation of man* through vital communion with God."[4] In other words, just as he had rejected a bare rationalistic formalism in ethics, so also Scheler rejected a formally rational system as the basis for religious knowledge.

Thus we see that when Scheler was doing a philosophy of religion,

---

[1] Cf. Collins, *op. cit.*, 183–90.
[2] *Ewigen*, 89–91; *Eternal*, 94–97.
[3] *Ewigen*, 92–99; *Eternal*, 93. See Collins, *op. cit.*, 190–93, for a careful critique of Scheler at this point.
[4] *Eternal*, 134. "Das Ziel der Religion ist nicht rationale Erkenntnis des Weltgrundes sondern das *Heil des Menschen* durch Lebensgemeinschaft mit Gott." *Ewigen*, 130.

he seemed to deny the dynamic vital participation element which he originally demanded of philosophy. Here he seemed to transfer the personal moral sphere (the "salvation of man") into the religious dimension exclusively. The term *philosophy* remains ambiguous, almost ambivalent. A formally rational philosophy is a purely theoretical, cognitive exercise, out of contact with the vital and the real. On the other hand a living philosophy of personal participation into being is salvational, religious knowledge. Yet this second type of philosophy almost seems to lose its essentially cognitive character. This ambiguity in the meaning of philosophy parallels the tensions that exist in being between spirit and life. Only at the end of his life did Scheler attempt to resolve these difficulties.

On May 5, 1928, Scheler published his last statement on the nature of philosophy, which he entitled significantly "Philosophical *Weltanschauung*." In this short but tightly condensed essay Scheler synthesized his last views on philosophy, anthropology and religion. Again, he established the autonomy of philosophy as distinct from a purely natural attitude to the world and from the three nineteenth-century aberrances of Positivism, Neo-Kantianism and Historicism. He stated that man is not free to choose whether or not he wants to develop a metaphysical idea and a metaphysical awareness. Man necessarily and always, consciously or unconsciously, *has* such an idea, such a feeling, acquired by himself or inherited from tradition. It belongs to the very essence of man to have the sphere of an abolute being before his thinking consciousness. All that man can actually choose for himself is a good and reasonable idea of the absolute or a poor and unreasonable idea. Thus, man can refuse to make for himself a clear idea of the absolute; he may even fill up the emptiness of his heart for the infinite with finite goods—money, country, a loved one. In this case, he creates an "idol" for himself.[1]

In this short study on the philosophical *Weltanschauung*, Scheler distinguished three types of knowledge. The first is the knowledge of achievement and of control, championed by the experimental, specialized sciences. The second he called "first philosophy," in the sense of both Aristotle and of Husserl. This is the discipline of pure phenomenology, a study of the direct insight into essences. While this calls for a "loving attitude," for the most part it is a rational study, removed from the existential and the vital. Scheler's categories remained very fluid. What he called "first philosophy" in 1928 seemed to possess many of

---

[1] *Weltanschauung*, 6–7; *Perspectives*, 2–3.

the same characteristics as the "purely philosophical metaphysics" of 1921.

The third type of knowledge, on the other hand, takes on religious, personal dimensions. It is called here metaphysical or salvational knowledge. This is no mere theoretical contemplation or "cerebral" exercise. This third type of knowledge involves the personal act and active commitment of man to God, to the extreme degree that God realizes his own essence in the free spiritual activity of man. The being of man is not only a primary access to God; man himself is a *microtheos*.[1] Many of the characteristics of this third type of salvational knowledge as explained in 1928 are closely related to Scheler's first definition of philosophy in 1916–17 as a love-determined act of participation by the core of an individual human person. In 1928 Scheler gave us a late synthesis of both his meaning of philosophy and his theory of being as united in the philosophy of man.

This exposition of Scheler's notion of philosophy is only introductory. Its purpose is primarily to catch the spirit and method of Scheler's philosophizing in order to see that his meaning for philosophy will largely control the content of his philosophy. More and more, Scheler came to see that all the major philosophical problems meet in the problem of man. With a phenomenological starting point in man, Scheler's final theory of man and being and God found its unity in man.

---

[1] *Weltanschauung*, 12–15; *Perspectives*, 9–12.

CHAPTER TWO

MAN AND METAPHYSICS

"MAN'S PLACE IN NATURE"

The study of man was always the architectonic study for Max Scheler. In 1927 he wrote:

> The questions "What is man?" and "What is man's place in the nature of things [*was ist seine Stellung im Sein?*]" have occupied me more deeply than any other philosophical question since the first awakening of my philosophical consciousness. Efforts of many years during which I have attacked this problem from all possible sides have come together.... I have had the good fortune to see that most of the philosophical work I had done previously has culminated in this study.[1]

This statement must not be taken to mean that this was a late discovery for Scheler. In a wide sense, all his early studies on the emotions and on ethics are not only descriptive psychological studies: they are attempts to isolate and identify the very being of man.

In 1915 Scheler stated in the essay "Towards the Idea of Man":

> From a certain understanding, all the central problems of philosophy lead back to the question what is man, what metaphysical place and position does he acquire within the totality of being, in respect to the world, in respect to God. With justice a number of older thinkers made the starting point of all philosophical questions "the place of man in the all"—an orientation concerning the metaphysical place for the essence of "man" and for his existence. ... All contemporary philosophy is filled with this complex of questions.[2]

Not only was "contemporary philosophy" concerned with the problem of man. Psychology, anthropology, history and biology, all held con-

---

[1] *Man's Place*, 3. "Die Fragen: (Was ist der Mensch, was ist seine Stellung im Sein?) haben mich seit dem ersten Erwachen meines philosophischen Bewusstseins wesentlicher und zentraler beschäftigt als jede andere philosophische Frage. Die langjährigen Bemühungen in denen ich von allen möglichen Seiten her das Problem umringte, haben sich ... zusammengefasst ..., und ich hatte das zunehmende Glück, zu sehen, dass der Grossteil aller Probleme der Philosophie, die ich schon behandelt, in dieser Frage mehr und mehr koinzidierten." *Stellung*, 7.

[2] "In einem gewissen Verstande lassen sich alle zentralen Probleme der Philosophie auf die Frage zurückführen, was der Mensch sei und welche metaphysische Stelle und Lage er innerhalb des Ganzen des Seins, der Welt und Gott einnehme. Nicht mit Unrecht pflegten eine Reihe älterer Denker die 'Stellung des Menschen im All' zum Ausgangspunkt aller philosophischen Fragestellung zu machen – d.h. eine Orientierung über den metaphysischen Ort des Wesens 'Mensch' und seiner Existenz, ... Die gesamte Philosophie der Gegenwart ist geradezu durchtränkt vom Sachverhalt dieser Frage. *Umsturz*, 173.

flicting views about man. Scheler announced that now phenomenology itself had also entered into the conflict over the meaning of man. His purpose from 1915 through 1928 was to make a phenomenological study of the "idea," the "essence," the "unity" of man, in order to discover the metaphysical dimensions of man.[1]

We have stated that Scheler's meaning and method of philosophy directly influenced the form and the content of his philosophical studies. We see that this is the case clearly and explicitly in his study of man. In the way that Husserl studied logic through phenomenology, Scheler attempted to make a phenomenological study of the "idea" and "essence" of man, independent from all the natural, social and psychological sciences. This was Scheler's explicit purpose in 1915.[2] In the 1927 work on man he rediscussed the techniques of phenomenology. A characteristic act of spirit is "the act of ideation" (der Akt der Ideierung) which is the grasping of the essential modes and the formal structures of the world. Such an insight into the essences of things is gained independently from contingently existing things and independently from an inductive number of individual cases. By way of an experiment, there is a "suspension of the reality-character of things" (versuchsweise – die Aufhebung des Wirklichkeitscharakters der Dinge). Man alone is capable of such a "spiritual" act.[3] And man's idea of man is gained only through such a series of reductions and "bracketings" which lead to an insight into the formal structure of the essence of man.

Scheler was well read not only in the social sciences but also in the biological and psychological sciences.[4] Yet he did not use their data in a purely scientific way. He confirmed these data (and all data) and employed them only within the total phenomenological grasp of man's essential nature.

The first step in the phenomenological method is the negative step of isolating a pure Phänomen, both from its purely fortuitous circumstances

---

[1] In 1927 Scheler himself instructed his readers how to follow the stages in his own developing views on man. In the Foreword to Stellung, he recommended this sequence of readings: 1) The essay "Towards the Idea of Man"; 2) Relevant passages in Formalism and in Sympathy; 3) "Man and History" (in Perspectives) and the volume Forms of Knowledge for the social consequences of this theory; 4) "The Forms of Knowledge and Culture" (from Perspectives); 5) "Man in the Era of Adjustment" (from Perspectives). See Stellung, 7–8. This outline, coming from Scheler himself, is an invaluable aid in our study. Meyerhoff in Perspectives rather arbitrarily edits Scheler's original text; he sees fit to relegate this very informative reflection of Scheler's to a footnote on page 97.

[2] Cf. "Vorbemerkung," Umsturz, 173–75.

[3] Stellung, 44–52; cf. Perspectives, 47–55. The translation of this phrase is our own.

[4] This is evident throughout his works, especially in Man's Place. In the late '20's he was even lecturing on the "Foundations of Biology" at Cologne. (This is a pertinent fact that the editor-translator of Perspectives completely omitted in the Author's Preface.) Cf. Stellung, 7.

and from all other related essential insights. In the study of man this means we must first clearly define *what man is not*. Such an act of isolating man's essence emphasizes the unique position of man's place in being and in nature. Ultimately, such a study will reveal the metaphysical dimensions of man's being and will show his relation to the Ground of Being.

In his early essay "Towards the Idea of Man," Scheler observed that for centuries the problem of man was to distinguish him from God, from pure spirits, from the angels. Modern science has changed the nature of the problem. We now must extricate man's unique essence from evolutionary modes of life and from brute animality.[1] Moreover, to the extent that modern science poses as the single, universal mode of knowledge, the problem of man becomes more crucial. At no time in history has man been so much of a problem to himself. Modern man for the first time is personally aware that he does not know *what* he is. Man needs courage to seek out the essential answers concerning man, while remaining detached from all the previous views of man. The philosophy of man can accept no untried, "unseen" views of man, however traditional the view may be.[2]

As we have seen, Scheler's method in the study of man is linked up with his purpose, namely, to explicate the *idea*, the *concept*, the *meaning* of man.[3] Many definitions of man are possible; many definitions of man have been actually devised and accepted by various cultures, within various stages of history. In "Man and History," Scheler described five basic types of man's conception of himself. The first conception of man was the theistic. According to this view, man was directly created by God, but man sinned and now must work out his religious salvation. The Greeks defined man in terms of his reason: man is a "rational animal," *homo sapiens*. A third meaning for man evolved from the naturalistic, positivistic and pragmatic sciences. Here man is defined as an animal who possesses only quantitative superiority in technical intelligence over the rest of the animal world. *Homo faber* in this context does not imply an essential difference between man and the brutes. The fourth idea of man according to this study by Scheler accepted the biological evolutionists at their word. Man is then seen to be the dead-end road to life itself, a *Sachgasse*, a biological weakling, a disease within the life process. Everything unique to man—reason,

---

[1] *Umsturz*, 175.
[2] *Stellung*, 7, 10; *Man's Place*, 4, 6. *Weltanschauung*, 62–63; *Perspectives*, 65–66.
[3] *Umsturz*, 173–76. *Stellung*, 9–11; *Man's Place*, 5–7.

freedom, spirit—restricts the Dionysian impulse towards complete vitalistic identification with life. The last concept of man Scheler discussed was the definition of man given by postulatory atheism. According to this idea, man's freedom, his responsibility, his very human existence demand the absence of God. Nietzsche's Superman is the prime example of this type of man.[1]

"Man and History" is light reading. Scheler intended it to be little more than a "warming up" exercise for his own philosophical anthropology. In *Man's Place* he retained only two of these five definitions of man as being actually influential in contemporary thought: the Jewish-Christian (theological) meaning of man and the Greek (philosophical) definition of man as a rational animal. But a new idea for man was introduced, the idea contributed by modern science and genetic psychology—the scientific definition of man as the highest, most complex stage of biological and psychological evolution.[2] Scheler's own anthropology has two goals. 1) It must extricate the unique essence of man within the context of natural science. 2) It must re-unite and combine the scientific concept of man with the theological and the philosophical. This second venture involved a corresponding shift in the theory of being. To achieve a totally unified idea of man, Scheler was forced to express his later views on anthropological pantheism.

Scheler was careful not to limit his definition of man too narrowly. If the unity of knowledge (and of being) were to be achieved in man, the definition of man's essence must be able to include all knowledge and all being. A general criticism of all previous conceptions of man was that each idea was too narrow and, in principle, each excluded the possibility of any further extension in meaning. Scheler's goal was to achieve a new unity in man through a concept of man which in principle synthesized all significant knowledge about man. Moreover, Scheler fully acknowledged the autonomy and the value of the non-human disciplines. We have seen that, late in life, he was engaged especially in the study of biology and comparative psychology. Only by acknowledging the full range of animal activity could the special level of man's being be appreciated. He loved to tell his students: "It is *difficult* to be man. Learn to know animals so that you will know how *difficult* it is to be man."[3]

In studying man's place in nature, Scheler replaced man within the

---

[1] *Weltanschauung*, 62–88; *Perspectives*, 65–93.

[2] *Stellung*, 9–11; *Man's Place*, 5–7.

[3] *Perspectives*, 26. "Es ist *schwer*, ein Mensch zu sein. 'Lernet die Tiere kennen, auf dass ihr merket, wie *schwer* es ist, ein Mensch zu sein.' – pflege ich meinen Studenten zu sagen." *Weltanschauung*, 28.

context of the material, the organic and the sentient. The result is that this 1927 study has much in common with Aristotle's study *On the Soul*.

Material things below the organic level have no inner-self-being. Their unity is nothing more than that of mutually interacting points of energy. Reflecting the indeterministic view of physics, Scheler was willing to accept the revolutionary doctrine that at the submicroscopic level all is chance and that *natural laws* at this level are purely structural laws of the human understanding (*Verstand*). Nevertheless, the inorganic world is very real. It resists ideal objectivization. The basic drive (*Drang*) exists here in its most primitive manifestation. Here, within centers of atomic energy lie the most powerful forces of all nature.[1] Scheler, a generation before the first splitting of the atom, had such a keen appreciation of scientific matters that he stood in reverent awe before even the inorganic.

"Psychic life" for Scheler in *Man's Place* suggests Aristotle's notion of *psyche*. It describes the lowest level of organic life. Living things possess the external, observable qualities of self-motion, self-formation, self-differentiation and a spatio-temporal self-limitation. Moreover, living things possess these qualities within their own intrinsic being, an ontic center—a for-and-in-themselves being (*ein Fürsich – und Innesein besitzen*). A certain inner community of being (*Seinsgemeinschaft*) is the most fundamental form of life, the psychic *Urphänomen* of life.[2] Inorganic bodies lack this "inner being" (*Innesein*).

A common vital impulse (*Gefühlsdrang*), a basic inner drive lies at the lowest levels of organic life. Scheler defended the special vital being of plants against both the pure mechanists (for whom all reality is physico-chemical) and against those who concede life only at the level of sensation and consciousness. The terms *"psychisch"* and *"seelisch"* are used interchangeably in *Man's Place* in describing the inner-structured life of plants. Plants have no central nervous system, no specific instincts (*Triebe*). There is only a basic drive (*Urdrang*) towards growth, reproduction and death. All the plant's needs—food, fertilization, environmental conditions—are *outside* the plant. Scheler described the condition by which a being's *Gefühlsdrang* is orientated to the *outside* as

---

[1] *Stellung*, 39–40, 61–62; *Man's Place*, 41–42, 66–68. Cf. Frings, *op. cit.*, ch. 2, "On the Bio-Psychic World," 31–48.
[2] *Stellung*, 11–12. Cf. *Man's Place*, 8. It is to be remembered that the translator also edited the text he chose to translate. Here an entire sentence has been omitted. (On p. vii the editor-translator explains that he has made a few omissions "for the sake of simplifying the text and the reading.")

"ecstatic," for in this respect it lacks inner-directedness. This first stage of life, the primaeval urge in things, is also present in its basic form in all animals and in man. The basic impulsive drive of organic life is one of the first objects of *resistance* we experience— it *resists* our objectivizing it into mere ideal concepts. This mark of resistance is the chief criterion to assure us of the ultimate *reality* of the thing.[1]

Instinct comprises the second level of the "ecstatic" life-impulse. Instincts are exclusively outer-directed without any conscious images. Scheler described six qualities of instinct very clearly and succinctly.[2] Instinct represents an increasing specialization of the vital impulse, but it is entirely and directly engaged with its *Umwelt*, the immediate environmental world.

The third stage of psychic life described by Scheler is that of *rote habit*. This type of habit is learned not by instinct but through repeated occurrences and retained by associated memory. Habit is gained through either self-training or conditioned training by another. The most common method of learning a habit is through the trial-and-error method. Habit, as a principle, creates a further qualitative enrichment of life, but at the animal level it can persist only through herd traditions.[3]

The fourth level of life is that of *practical intelligence*. Like Dewey, Scheler defined intelligence as the power of making a meaningful response in the face of a new situation. The perception of the inter-relatedness of the complex of affairs within the situation results in the experience which Köhler described as the "Aha! experience." Scheler strongly defended Köhler's conclusions that animals are fully capable of simple, intelligent behavior. Animals are capable of using simple instruments and of perceiving a cause-effect phenomenon in its actual dynamic function. The evolutionist-pragmatic view of man as *homo faber* never essentially transcends the level of practical intelligence. According to this view, man is quantitatively superior in his intelligence, but there is not present a genuinely new phenomenon, an essentially new order of being. The difference between a clever

---

[1] *Stellung*, 12–16; *Man's Place*, 9–14.

[2] These qualities are: 1) An instinct must be meaningful and purposeful for the whole of the living organism. 2) It must act according to a definite unchanging rhythm 3) It is rigid and typical in its responses to a situation; its responses are geared for the good of the species. 4) An instinct is innate and hereditary. 5) It is unlearned: it is complete and perfect with its first use. 6) It acts without representations, images, or ideas of any kind. *Stellung*, 16–23; *Man's Place*, 14–21.

[3] *Stellung*, 23–29; *Man's Place*, 21–29.

chimpanzee and Edison (Scheler's favorite example) is only a difference of degree.[1]

Animals do more than possess the "inner being" of plants. They also
have sensation and consciousness, along with a central organization by
which they receive and retain reports concerning their situation in the
environmental world. Only with the phenomenon of *spirit* do we reach
the level that is distinctively and essentially *human*. With the presence
of spirit in man, man has a most special place in nature, for spirit is
evidence of a being that is essentially distinct from all forms of life.

SPIRIT AND PERSON

Scheler's most detailed exposition of the meaning and activity of
spirit appeared in *Man's Place*. This is the main source of our present
remarks.

The element of spirit completely transcends the competence of
biology and psychology. It is not just a higher order of life; it is a
genuinely new phenomenon which cannot be derived from the natural
evolution of life. Spirit possesses two essential characteristics. It has the
power of objectifying the *real* environmental world through knowledge
in intentionality and in symbolic interpretation of that world. In man,
it possesses the power of objectifying its own physiological and psychological states, all of its psychic experiences and vital functions.[2] This,
then, is a consciousness of the *I*, in which the *I* is an object of knowledge.
As we shall continue to see, self-consciousness becomes a technical term
for Scheler. The knowledge of the *I* is our knowledge of the Self.

The act of objectifying the pockets of resistance which make up the
real world is also called the act of "ideation." This was described by
Scheler in *Man's Place* in phenomenological terms. Ideation is an act
essentially superior to mere practical intelligence. Ideation means to
grasp the essential modes and the formal structures of the world.
Ideation allows an original insight into the essences of things. This act
requires not only a tentative suspension of reality; it requires an actual

---

[1] *Stellung*, 29–36; *Man's Place*, 29–37. Scheler's usual word is *Intelligenz* or *praktische Intelligenz*. Very occasionally he will use *Intellekt* in this sense. The meaning of these terms must be
carefully distinguished from his meaning for *Geist*. For a comparison of Scheler with Dewey
on this point of intelligence, cf. *Intelligence in the Modern World: John Dewey's Philosophy*,
edited, with an introduction by Joseph Ratner (New York: The Modern Library, 1939),
ch. VII, "Intelligence in Social Action," 435–66. This is a series of very carefully selected
texts. Also, cf. W. Koehler, *The Mentality of Apes*, translated by E. Winter (New York: Har-
court, Brace and Co., 1926).

[2] *Stellung*, 37–39; *Man's Place*, 39–40.

opposition to the vitalistic impulse of the real. Man becomes the "being who can say No !'" (*Neinsagenkönner*), "the ascetic of life," "the eternal protester" against life. This attitude of denial becomes, in turn, the moral condition for the upsurge (*Aufschwung*) of spirit to true philosophical knowledge. Therefore, through spirit, man is no longer caught "ecstatically" within the situational complex of his environmental world. Man is freed from his environment. By the act of objectifying the *real* world, man creates his own ideal world and remains unlimitedly open to the world.

These distinctive spiritual acts of man were described by Scheler as the basis for further acts specific to man. Man alone develops the permanent, unifying categories of thing and substance. Only man lives, from the beginning of his existence, within a unified space dimension. Man can think of empty space and of abstract quantity. Thus, man has the capacity for spontaneous movement and action, according to a definite order, within the infinite emptiness of his space-time dimension. In science (the scientific *Weltanschauung*) man can structurally form the objective world, impose laws upon it (the "Natural laws" of the physicists) and gain effective control over nature (the knowledge of control). At the same time, the term *spirit* does not refer only to knowledge activities. Spirit also performs such voluntary and emotional acts, as kindness, love, reverence, wonder, bliss.[1]

Spirit transcends space and time. While indirectly dependent upon and imbedded in the lower vital impulse, spirit is in no way *evolved from* the lower order and cannot be *reduced to* it. Indeed, spirit arises only in its opposition to life. It achieves its higher level of being only by dialectically contradicting the very bases of its own reality. Scheler compared this process to Freud's theory of sublimation. At this time, Scheler understood Freud to mean that through the repression of the lower instinctual drives, spirit sublimates the lower energy into spiritual activity. Scheler consistently criticized this theory of Freud, as he understood it, for its reduction of spiritual phenomena to the vital and for its failure to account for the essentially distinct phenomena of spirit. Nevertheless, Scheler continued to employ a similar explanation of repression and sublimation in his own descriptions of spiritual phenomena.

The second essential activity of spirit is that man can reflectively

---

[1] *Stellung*, 34–52; *Man's Place*, 35–55. In the Editor's Introduction in *Sympathy*, p. xxiv, Stark seems to overlook Scheler's meaning of "psychic life" as being co-relative with biological life. At the "psychic"—biological—level, man is at one with the rest of nature. Stark correctly interprets Scheler's theory of spirit and person in the subsequent discussion (xxv–xxx).

consider his own vital functions as objects of knowledge and objects of strictly scientific investigation. Man's very inner psychological and psychic states can become *objects* of knowledge. This is man's knowledge of the *I*. Spiritual acts, however, cannot be objectified. This is a key doctrine in Scheler's whole theory of spirit and person. Spirit is pure actuality, in the sense that its very being is to be engaged in activity. And, as Scheler stated in *Man's Place*, "the center of actions in which spirit appears within a finite mode of being we call 'person.'"[1] A preliminary understanding of Scheler's definition of person is necessary at this point.

In *Man's Place*, Scheler's discussion of person was set within a biological-psychological study and heavily grounded in metaphysical principles. In contrast to this, the entire second half of *Formalism* (first published in 1916, but completed by 1914) was devoted to the phenomenological exposition of the meaning of person within an ethical context. In *Formalism*, Scheler defended the ethical value of person against formal, rationalistic systems (especially, that of Kant) and against purely scientific, psychological descriptions of persons. For all the differences in context, the formal definitions of person given in *Man's Place* agreed favorably with those previously given in *Formalism*. Thus, in one passage in *Man's Place* Scheler wrote:

> Spirit is the only being incapable of becoming an object. It is pure actuality. It has being only in and through the execution of its acts. The center of spirit, the person, is not an object or a substantial kind of being, but a continuously self-executing, ordered structure of acts. The person is only in and through his acts.[2]

In *Formalism* Scheler stated:

> *Person is, in its own essence, the concrete unity of being for essentially different kinds of acts;* which [this concrete unity] in itself (not therefore in respect to us) precedes all essential differences in acts (especially, then, the differences between outer and inner perception, outer and inner willing, outer and inner feeling and loving, hating, etc.). *The being of the person "is the foundation for" all essentially different acts.*[3]

---

[1] *Man's Place*, 36. "Das Akzentrum aber, in dem Geist innerhalb endliches Seinssphären erscheint, bezeichnen wir als 'Person.'" *Stellung*, 35.

[2] *Man's Place*, 47. "Der Geist ist das einzige Sein, das selbst Gegenstand unfähig ist, – er ist reine Aktualität, hat sein Sein nur im freien Vollzug seiner Akte. Das Zentrum des Geistes, die 'Person,' ist weder gegenständliches, noch dingliches Sein, sondern nur ein stetig selbst sich vollziehendes (wesenhaft bestimmtes) Ordnungsgefüge von Akten. Die Person ist nur in ihren Akten und durch sie." *Stellung*, 44–45.

[3] "*Person ist die konkrete, selbst wesenhafte Seinseinheit von Akten verschiedenartigen Wesens*, die an sich (nicht also *pros emas*) allen wesenhaften Aktdifferenzen (insbesondere auch der Differenz äusserer und innerer Wahrnehmung, äusserem und innerem Wollen, äusserem und innerem Fühlen und Lieben, Hassen, usw.) vorhergeht. *Das Sein der Person 'fundiert' alle wesenhaft verschiedenen Akte.*" *Formalismus*, 393–94.

Scheler explained further that person is not merely an empty "starting point" of acts, but the concrete being (*das konkrete Sein*) in which all acts have their actual, real connection. Another passage of *Formalism* reads:

Person can *never* be thought of as a *thing* or a *substance*, which somehow has faculties or powers, nor thereby is it a "faculty" or a "power" of reason, and so on. Rather, person is the immediate co-experiencing *unity* of a living experience—not a bare thing concluded to as being beyond and outside the immediate experience. ... Every finite person is an *individual* and he *himself* is this as a *person*.[1]

These are excellent phenomenological descriptions, with all the inherent clarity and weaknesses of Scheler's bare phenomenological intuition. It will allow no discussion about notions that are not immediately experienced. It asks for no further causal explanation for the intuited essence. Person, then, is experienced as being the unified, concrete center for those experiencing-acts that are essentially distinct from the lower vital functions of the psychophysiological organism.

For Scheler, three essential characteristics were included in the definition of person. 1) Person appears only as the phenomena of spirit. 2) Person and its acts cannot be objectified. 3) Persons are individualized through their own intrinsic constitution. We have already discussed *spirit* and its essential activities. We have seen that the integration of these spiritual activities into a centralized unity makes up the very constitution of the person.

The term *act* (*Akt*) was used by Scheler in a highly specialized sense to refer only to *spiritual acts*. As we shall see, *acts* are sharply distinguished from *functions* (*Funktionen*). Acts in their most essential nature transcend the body. They were characterized by Scheler as being "psychophysiologically indifferent" to the spatio-temporal conditions of the body. Acts belong to the person, originate from within the person and are projected *into* time. "It belongs to the essence of the reality of acts that they are themselves experienced only in performance [*Vollzug*]."[2] The full understanding of the meaning and the reality of an *act* precludes all possibility of it becoming an intentional object.

As we have seen, spirit achieves its essential transcendence over the lower levels of life through the acts by which it resists and represses the impulses of life and objectifies all lower reality in the act of ideation.

[1] "Person *niemals* als ein *Ding* oder eine *Substanz* gedacht werden darf, die irgendwelche Vermögen oder Kräfte hätte, darunter ein 'Vermögen' oder eine 'Kraft' der Vernunft usw. Person ist vielmehr die unmittelbar miterlebte *Einheit* des Er-lebens – nicht ein nur gedachtes Ding hinter und ausser dem unmittelbar Erlebten. ... Jede endliche Person ein *Individuum* ist und dies als *Person selbst*." *Formalismus*, 382.

[2] "Es gehört zum Wesen des Seins von Akten, nur in Vollzug selbst erlebt gegeben zu sein." *Ibid.*, 385.

This is an act of pure knowledge. Consistent with his views on the meaning of a purely rational philosophy, Scheler's meaning for ideal knowledge had almost a pejorative sense. The strict knowledge-act objectifies reality into formal, essential structures, while suspending it from the existential impulse of things. Scheler's word for *object* in this context is the German word *Gegenstand*. This term, along with all its derivatives, preserves its rigidly cognitive-intentional references. It must be carefully distinguished from an objectivity that refers to the real extra-intentional world.

Scheler declared in *Formalism* that a spiritual act itself cannot be objectified in the knowledge act (*niemals aber ist ein Akt auch ein Gegenstand*). This principle is an important link in his whole theory of man, knowledge and being. Not even by reflection upon an act can that act be objectified. Reflection upon an act gives a type of knowledge in "accompanying" ("*begleitet*") the act and in re-living the experiencing of the act, but this is not a case of true objectification.

Scheler's doctrine here agreed with his views on epistemology and metaphysics. He firmly refused to reduce philosophy and reality to mere ideal abstractions. Love and value responses are more immediate and authentic modes of participation (*Teilnehmen*) into reality than abstract knowledge. Scheler's phenomenology had as one of its ends to gain insight into the essences of values and into the content of our emotional experiences. Therefore, while spiritual acts cannot be perceived and objectified into idealized structures, they can be studied through phenomenology. In this case, we can come to "know" the act by co-performing it (*Mitvollzug*), or performing it previous to or subsequent to the act itself. This is the only way we know our own spiritual acts and (as we shall see) this is the only way in which we can participate in the acts of other persons. This is by no means a lesser type of knowledge, but it is an essentially different or non-objectifying mode of participating in the full reality of spiritual acts.

If spirit and its acts cannot be objectified, then neither can person be converted into an object, for person is nothing more than the centralized unity constituted in its own spiritual acts.

But if an act is never an object, so then very properly the living *person* in his act-performance is also never an object. The only and the exclusive kind of its "being-given" is only in *its very performance itself* (also even in the performance of the reflection upon its own acts)—its performance, in which it experiences itself in an immediate, living way. Or, where one deals with other persons: a co-performance, re-performance or a pre-performance of their acts. Also in such cases ... the acts of the other persons have not been objectified.[1]

It is evident that the application of the principle of non-objectification of other persons and their acts will have important bearing upon much of our later discussion on the problem of persons living in community. The third essential characteristic of person for Scheler which we have singled out was that each person contained within itself its own principle of individuation. Since person in the essential constitution of its own essence transcends the body, then the body in its space-time dimensions cannot account for the individuation of the person. The concrete center of spiritual acts which makes up the person is already individualized through itself and in itself. We shall see how this discussion over the principle of individuation returns frequently in the social problems considered in *Sympathy*. The very fact of the multiplicity of individual spirits (persons) will allow the possibility for community relations to develop among persons.[2]

In *Formalism*, Scheler defended the true moral autonomy of the person against Kant's "law-rule" (*Logonomie*) by pure reason.[3] The moral person is more than a mere "being of reason" (*Vernunftwesen*) or a "person of reason" (*Vernunftperson*).[4] Person can neither be objectified nor can it serve as the mere logical subject of a proposition. The full meaning of Scheler's teaching on person becomes clearer when person is contrasted with the *I*.

---

[1] "Ist aber schon ein Akt niemals Gegenstand, so ist erst recht niemals Gegenstand die in ihrem Aktvollzug lebende *Person*. Die einzige und ausschliessliche Art ihrer Gegebenheit ist vielmehr allein ihr *Aktvollzug selbst* (auch noch der Aktvollzug ihrer Reflexion auf ihrer Akte) – ihr Aktvollzug, in dem lebend sie gleichzeitig sich erlebt. Oder, wo es sich um andere Personen handelt: Mit- oder Nachvollzug oder Vorvollzug ihrer Akte. Auch in solchem Mitresp. Nachvollzug und Vorvollzug der Akte einer anderen Person steckt nichts von Vergegenständlichung." *Ibid.*, 397. Parallel to this thought is the following passage in *Man's Place*: (Our own translation). "To the being of our own Person we can only collect ourselves, to it we can only concentrate ourselves—but we cannot objectify it. Also other persons, as persons, are not able to be objectified. ... We can win a knowing participation with them only in so far as we perform their free acts after and with them, which is called by the poor term "discipleship"; or through a possible "understanding" in the attitude of spiritual love, which is the total opposite of all objectification, that is, as we are accustomed to say, that we identify ourselves with the willing, with the love of a person—and thereby with him himself." *Stellung*, 45; cf. *Man's Place*, 47–48.

[2] *Weltanschauung*, 34, 126, n. 19; *Perspectives*, 33, 132, n. 19.

[3] *Formalismus*, 382–83.

[4] The term *Vernunft* for Scheler implied a bare theoretical power of abstract thought. It had its immediate source in Kant's doctrine on reason, but also has reference to the *homo sapiens* of the Greeks. Most of Scheler's references to *Vernunft* are made in a depreciating sense. *Formalismus*, 383, ff.

PERSON AND 'I'

Spirit, its acts, and the person can never become objects. The *I* (*Ich*), on the other hand, is by definition always an object (*Gegenstand*). The individual *I* is the object of inner perception.[1] In this case, we speak of someone perceiving his own *I*.[2] The *I*, its appearances (*Erscheinungen*), and its contents (*Inhalte*) fall under the observation of science and psychology as common objects of knowledge. This class of objects are called *functions* (*Funktionen*), and, as we have remarked, functions must be carefully distinguished from *acts*.

All *functions* are functions of the psychophysiological unity which constitutes the *I*. Functions necessarily entail a body and the environmental world. Functions are facts which occur in the phenomenal space-time sphere: they are observable and measurable in space-time quantities. Seeing, hearing, testing, vital feelings are examples of functions.[3]

Scheler placed much importance upon the contrast between person and *I*, between acts and functions. The *I* and its functions fall within the competence of modern experimental psychology. In this context, Scheler was prepared to discuss at great length the findings of psychology. But since person and acts cannot be converted into objects of knowledge, they can be known only through the peculiar investigations of phenomenology by which one can "accompany" his inner acts in order to "intuit" the real "essence" of that act.

Functions can be related to acts in two ways. A function can become the object of an act; e.g., a person can reflectively consider what "seeing" is. Also, functions can serve as the means by which acts are directed to other objects. For instance, when a man sees the beating of a drum and hears the sound of the drum, he makes the *act* of judgment that this complex state of affairs (*Sachverhalt*) is really a single fact, that what he sees and what he hears is the same thing.

[1] Scheler also distinguished between the individual *I* and a general *I* (*Ichheit*). The latter is the object of a "formless intuition" (*formloser Anschauung*). This term recurs very infrequently. It seems to refer to a type of unspecified knowledge about the *I* in general.

[2] It is to be noted that we retain the English term *I* as the literal translation of Scheler's use of *Ich* here in *Formalism*. We avoid the term *Ego* because of its psychological and psychoanalytic connotations. We also avoid a reverting to a more common idiom in English whereby the reflexive case of *I* is rendered as *me* or *self*; for example, we may speak of someone perceiving himself or of someone perceiving his Self (*cf. infra* n. 35). German has the same usage. Yet Scheler deliberately speaks of perceiving the *I* (*Ich*), not of perceiving the Self (*Selbst*). Therefore, for clarity and precision of thought, we will abide exactly by the Schelerian terms. As we shall see in the following chapter, further difficulties will arise in the study of *Sympathy*.

[3] *Formalismus*, 397–98.

Functions are immediately complete and perfect; acts carry with them a meaning, an intentionality and a type of symbolic reference that demand further interpretation. For example, every personal act has a past and a future. What is "past" and what is "future" as experienced within a personal act, has an "essence" knowable only through phenomenological investigations. However, one can relive the past and plan the future only through a series of psychophysiological functions that take place in the present. These functions, in turn, can become the object of scientific study; e.g., for instance, science can study the amount of electrical energy discharged in the brain while a subject plans the future. But science can never uncover the personal dimensions of acts themselves; science can never know what "the future" means to a person.[1]

The *I* for Scheler is always the experienced *I* (*Erlebnis-ich*), that is, it is always an object of thought or of feeling. Only a person can be the subject which performs acts (*handelt*). This led Scheler to reconstruct our common language. It is not entirely correct to say that "I go for a walk." Only a person can initiate the activity of walking. In this case, the *I* in the sentence stands for both the grammatical meaning of "first person," and also for the singular concrete human being who is performing the act. Hence, the same is true when I say, "I am perceiving myself." Here again, the *I* does not designate the psychical *I*; it merely designates a man (*Mensch*), who has an *I* and who is conscious of his *I* as the same person in the performance of his outer and inner perceptions. *Myself* remains ambiguous. Does it refer to an inner perception of the psychical *I*, or does it merely refer to an outer perception of the *body-I* (*Leib-ich*)? On the other hand, when I say, "I am perceiving my *I*," then I clearly announce that I have an inner perception of the psychical *I* as the object of my perception.[2]

The body is always perceived within its environmental world (*Umwelt*). The *I* is necessarily related to the outer world. One part of the outer world for the *I* is its own body (*Leib*). In the fully unified experience of the *I* and its body there is constituted in all its intrinsic, essential relatedness a single unity which Scheler called the *body-I* (*Leib-ich*). He further distinghuished between the living body (*Leib*) and the body as an inanimate thing (*Körper*). He denied that we first

---

[1] *Ibid.*, 424.
[2] *Ibid.*, 400; also, 97. In itself, spirit transcends the human situation. The definition of person as the center of spiritual acts can be applied to God and angels as well as to man. Man is a *human* person, a person-in-body, a person who experiences his own *I*. The *I*, then, is experienced, objectified knowledge, i.e., reflective and scientific knowledge about man.

become aware of our own body through external perception, as if it were an inanimate object (*Körper*), detached and separate from us. Rather, the living body (*Leib*) is intrinsically and essentially related to all the *I*-functions as an essential component of all the body-*I* experiences. Functions such as hearing, tasting, touching take place within the total living body experiences. Yet if I touch the smoothness of silk, it is not necessary for me to perceive beforehand my own finger, as if it were an inanimate object touching silk. I merely feel the smoothness of silk through the unified body-*I* experience. All subsequent learning of a human person continues within the background of the most basic intentional constitution of its body-*I* relation.[1]

These distinctions in respect to the primary objects of our experience will play a crucial role in the discussion concerning our perception if the alien *I*. At the same time, they allowed Scheler to discuss in great detail the relevant psychological studies dealing with man, consciousness, perception, sensation and the emotions.[2] But all the while, he preserved the transcendence of the person. Most important to the context of *Formalism*, he defended the role of person as being the only bearer of genuine ethical values.

The *I* is also distinguished from person by way of its relatedness to the world. While the *I* is intrinsically and essentially related to the outer environmental world, especially in its body-*I* constitution, person constitutes its own world and stands endlessly open before its world. Person is, by definition, individual and concrete, so that the corresponding world for each person is equally individual and concrete. As every spiritual act belongs to an individual person, so also very intentional object (*Gegenstand*) is essentially constituted as "belonging" to an individual world. Person is not a part of a world, not even part of its own world; the person is merely the correlate (*Korrelate*) of a "world"— the world in which it fulfills its own experiences. In this sense, both the person and its corresponding world are something absolute; they have no intrinsic relation to an outside world or to an alien *I*. God, for example, the Person of Persons, essentially has no outside world and no intrinsic relatedness to some other *I* in community. The *I*, however, as we have seen, is necessarily related to both the outside world and to an alien *I*.[3]

---

[1] *Ibid.*, 408–13.
[2] The pages from 413 through 485 of *Formalismus* contain a close study of contemporary psychological studies.
[3] *Ibid.*, 403–05.

MAN THE MICROCOSM

The major questions of metaphysics were never far from Scheler's active mind. Not only questions of epistemology, but also all the questions of ethics, of values, of work, of sociology and of religion found their basic ground in the answers concerning the Ground of Being. In the most general sense Scheler's metaphysics can be described as realistic, but non-causal. The most crucial questions for Scheler involved the resolution of the dualism between life and spirit. More and more Scheler came to realize that his metaphysics was inseparably intertwined with his philosophy (his phenomenology) of man. In short, the aim of his late philosophical anthropology was to combine the scientific, philosophical and theological definitions of man into a single, unified meaning, consonant with his definition of being itself. Man became a microcosm not only of the scientific and philosophical world; man also contained within himself the whole of the theological world: man became the *microtheos*.

A statement of Scheler's metaphysics is difficult. First of all, there is some ambiguity inherent in the very meaning and use of the term *metaphysics*. Metaphysics, for Scheler, suffered the same fate of fluctuating in meaning as we have seen in his definition of philosophy. Also, it is precisely within the realm of the metaphysics of being that Scheler's most radical intellectual development took place.

In general, there are within being the two most basic categories of the *real* and the *ideal*. The *real* is the contingently existential (*Dasein*), with its underlying ground of dynamic, vital impulse. Its reality is verified epistemologically by its crude resistance to ideal objectification. In referring to reality, Scheler makes no distinction between the German words *Realität* and *Wirklichkeit*. *Ideal* being is the realm of intentional being, the realm of essences, the realm of intentional objects—*Gegenstände*. Ideal being is accessible only to spirit. Spirit, therefore, must deny and withstand the impulses of the real to consider *objectively*—in knowledge—the pure essences of things. This is a more refined statement of the first moral condition—asceticism—for philosophical knowledge.

A pure, abstract study of metaphysics would consider the formal, essential structure of bare ontological being, a neutral being which in itself need be neither *real* nor *ideal*. For Scheler, this is a phenomenological study that begins with the first essential insight that something is—*is* in an ontological sense. Complete investigation of this insight will unveil the further essential relations and complexes within all possible being. For example, in "The Nature of Philosophy" Scheler explained that our first insight into limited being leads—in thought—to the necessity that there be a final ground in Absolute Being.[1] Ten years later in *Man's Place* Scheler was involved in the same phenomenological exercise. Here he stated that consciousness of the world, self-consciousness, and the (formal) consciousness of God are essentially, necessarily related. These three form "an inseparable structural unity."[2] However, in 1927 Scheler's intellectual development made him see a new significance and relevance for these insights. He then declared that the unity and relatedness of mental being must be predicated of *reality* itself.

Scheler's first philosophical interests dealt with ethics and methodology. As we have seen, from his first work on *Logical and Ethical Principles*, he declared that ethical values are derived by man through a separate intentional experience from that by which we discover logical principles. In *Formalism* he vigorously attacked Kant's ethics (and all rationalistics systems) which in principle derive ethical values exclusively from formal, intellectual considerations. Scheler's defense of Pascal's "order of the heart" in describing the *a priori* hierarchy of emotional values was to give proper credit to the world of emotions, of drives and impulses. Life-and-emotional values put man in direct contact with the real, with the vital and the concrete. A philosophical study of this dimension of man (in the sense of phenomenology) seeks to gain direct insight into the pure "essences" of values. Such a study does not abstract the realm of values into purely cognitive idealizations; its goal is to describe the intentional content within the concrete experiencing act as it responds to its own intrinsic ends (*Ziele*). Response to material values puts man into direct contact with the vital, the *real*. This impulsive vital drive, for Scheler, is the basic core of reality. The different levels of reality, the inorganic, the vegetative, the sentient and the spiritual, all respond to this vital drive according to their own degree of being. But each level of being must remain in vital communion with this basic drive. The fault of rationalism is that by an act of super-intellectualization it loses contact with the material and the vital. Scheler proposed a "re-sublimation" to allow man a rational return to the vital sources of his being.[3]

We have already noted Scheler's changes of mind in defining the

---

[1] Cf. *Ewigen*, 93–99; *Eternal*, 98–104.
[2] Cf. *Man's Place*, 89–90. "Welt-, Selbst-, und Gottesbewusstsein bilden eine unzerreissbare Struktureinheit." *Stellung*, 82.
[3] Cf. "Man in the Era of Adjustment" in *Perspectives*, 94–126; *Weltanschauung*, 89–118.

meaning of philosophy. In 1916–17 he made the act of philosophizing a love-impelled activity of the whole person. However, in 1921, while writing on the philosophy of religion, Scheler carefully restricted formal metaphysical knowledge to a purely abstract body of theoretical truths as proposed by the rationalists. Such a "metaphysical" knowledge is only in possession of cognitive, *ideal* being. It gives only *rational* knowledge of the basis of the world; it reveals the "cerebral god of the intellectuals." On the other hand, it is *religious* experience (originally a group experience) that puts one into vital communion with Absolute Being in its real, dynamic dimension. This involves a personal commitment to and active participation with Absolute Being. This type of knowledge is "salvational."[1] At the end of his life, Scheler (having lost his Catholic faith) re-united *metaphysics* itself with salvational knowledge.[2] The reason for this transition in thought is twofold. In the realm of being itself he had to resolve the idealism-realism problem within the context of his own devising. Secondly, at this time, he sought explicitly to synthesize the major philosophical questions within the philosophy of *man*.

In man, the problem of realism-idealism is not the relation between body and soul, between matter and form, between extension and thought. It is the relation of the most basic *vital impulse* as opposed to *spirit*. Scheler spoke of *Drang, Lebensdrang* or *Gefühlsdrang* to describe this most basic *reality* in things. The inorganic world possesses this inherent dynamism in its resistance to destruction and in all its forms of physical and chemical power (kinetic and potential). Vegetative life, the brutes, men are individualized centers of this same basic impulse. The higher grades of life possess more highly centralized and organized centers of activity.

In the most basic sense of bare existence, the material and the organic are the most elemental and most powerful forces in man and in being. The primitive drives for self-preservation, towards nourishment and reproduction form the rock-bottom foundation for all the higher phenomena of spirit.[3] Scheler agress with Nicolai Hartmann that the

---

[1] *Ewigen*, 129–30; *Eternal*, 133–34.

[2] Cf. the 1925 address, "The Forms of Knowledge and Culture" for a definition of knowledge identical with the 1916–17 definition. Knowledge is a "love," a relation of being (*ein Seinsverhältnis*), a participation of one being into the circumstantial existence of another (*das Verhältnis des Teilhabens eines Seienden am Sosein eines anderes Seienden*). Cf. *Perspectives*, 39–40; *Weltanschauung*, 40.

[3] Scheler's reaction to Freud is very interesting. He understands Freud to describe the origin of higher cultural and humanistic ideals in man—elements of *spirit*—through a special type of repression of the lower drives through the process of *sublimation*. Scheler criticizes this theory of Freud on two counts. 1) Scheler asks: what converts an unhealthy *repression* into a

higher values are weaker than the lower values and that the higher levels of life and spirit are dependent upon the lower. Spirit in its objectifying activity totally transcends the temporal and the spatial. Yet it subsists in and depends on the more basic life forces for bare survival. Spirit's relationship to life is similar to some traditional explanation of the soul's dependence upon the body.

> The spiritual act is indirectly dependent in so far as it requires energy, upon the temporal processes of life and is, as it were, embedded in them.[1]

Pure spirit without this life-impulse may be conceivable theoretically, but it would literally be lifeless and unreal. Therefore, Scheler was forced to reject all forms of theistic creationism which hold pure spirit, as *spirit*, to be omnipotently effective. Only the reverse is true. The life-impulse itself is power, thrust, drive. This is absolutely primary and basic. Only within this life-drive does spirit emerge and develop by an activity which dialectically receives its impulse only from the life-force it opposes.

The phenomenon of spirit arises originally only in the experience of man. Scheler was making a phenomenological description of man's experience of himself and the world.

> The process of becoming human represents the highest sublimation known to us and, at the same time, the most intimate fusion of all the essential stages of nature. For man unifies within himself all the essential stages of existence [*des Daseins*], especially of life.[2]

From this starting point (man is a microcosm), Scheler built his own theory of being. He was conscious of the disastrous results of a Cartesian dualism both in man and in being. From man's experience of himself as a perfectly unified being, Scheler declared that the ultimate metaphysical Ground is also one. Though man experiences within himself, the tugs and pulls of vital drives, along with the higher activity of spirit (the eternal conflict of the two "laws" within us), man is *one* being with the two attributes irreducible to each other—impulse and spirit. From

---

healthy *sublimation*, unless there is admitted a prior spiritual element which does the "sublimating" in the first place? 2) Freud would have spirit to evolve automatically from the lower level of being. Scheler's "ascetic" denial of the impulsive is very similar to his own interpretation of Freud's theory of sublimation. But Scheler will vigorously defend the prior independent realm of spirit and will deny that the higher (spirit) can ever evolve from the lower.

[1] *Man's Place*, 81. "Nur indirekt ist der geistige Akt, sofern er Tätigkeit beansprucht, auch abhängig von einem zeitlichen Lebensvordrang und gleichsam in ihm eingebettet." *Stellung*, 74.

[2] *Man's Place*, 69–70. "Die Menschwerdung, wie ich schon sagte, die uns bekannte höchste Sublimierung – und zugleich die innigste Einigung aller Wesensregionen der Natur dar. Denn der Mensch fasst alle Wesensstufen des Daseins überhaupt, insbesondere des Lebens in sich zusammen." *Stellung*, 64.

this evidence, Scheler declared that the ultimate Ground of Being is also one, but one that has two distinct attributes, two distinct B lines of progress, two dimensions of being, accessible and describable by man only by two distinct intentional modes of description.

Scheler's final theory of being emerged slowly. The need for unity forced him to combine the vitalistic and spiritual elements. Many isolated statements are extreme and seem to maintain a pan-vitalistic monism, with the realm of spirit being a late and superfluous appendage. The category of the *real* seems more basic than that of the *ideal*. But the realm of spirit, of higher values, of freedom, remains an intrinsic component of man's experience and an essential factor of being itself. Ultimately, these factors must be united in the World-ground.

> In our metaphysics (there is) in the spirit of the *one* substantial divine World-ground the two attributes known to us, "Spirit" and "Drive."[1]

Here Scheler declares that there is one World-ground with two known attributes, spirit and drive, *Geist* und *Drang*.

> According to our metaphysics the *realization of Spirit* in the divine substance, eternally positing itself through *drive*, the second attribute of divinity known to us, and the *ideation of drive* ("the spiritualization of life") are both the *same* metaphysically identical process, viewed one time from the point of view of "Spirit" and "Essence" and the second time from the point of view of "Drive" and "Concrete Existence (*Dasein*)." World history is for us the cultural, temporal manifestation of the relaxed tension between the basic opposition of Spirit and Drive (*natura naturans*) in a functional unity of the World-ground and thus also the mutual interpenetration of Spirit and Power.[2]

> Spirit and drive, the two attributes of being, apart from their growing mutual interpenetration—their intrinsic end (*Ziel*)—are not complete in themselves. They grow within themselves in their manifestation in the history of the human spirit and in the evolution of life in the world.[3]

---

[1] (Our own translation.)"In unserer Metaphysik ... im Geiste des gotthaften *einen* substantialen Weltgrundes mit den zwei uns bekannten Attributen, 'Geist' und 'Drang'." *Weltanschauung*, 123, n. 15. Cf. *Perspectives*, 130. The long footnotes to this essay on knowledge and culture in this work contain very valuable, technical metaphysical points. Unfortunately, the translation in *Perspectives* does not handle these technical passages very successfully.

[2] (Our own translation.) "Nach unserer Metaphysik sind *Realisierung des Geistes* in der göttlichen, sich ewig selbst setzenden Substanz durch das Zweite uns bekannte Attribut der Gottheit, durch den *Drang*, und *Ideierung des Dranges* (Vergeisterung des Lebens') nur *ein* metaphysisch-*identischer* Progress, das eine Mal von 'Geist' and 'Wesen,' das zweite Mal von 'Drang' und 'Dasein' aus gesehen. Die Weltgeschichte ist uns die bildhafte zeitliche Manifestation der Entspannung des Urgegensatzes von Geist und Drang (natura naturans) im funktionell einheitlichen Weltgrund, und damit auch die *gegenseitige Durchdringung* von Geist und Macht. *Weltanschauung*, 124, n. 16. Cf. *Perspectives*, 131. This is a fine summary-statement of Scheler's recognition of a basic dualism in being—*Urgegensatz von Geist und Drang*—and its resolution—*Entspannung*—through the mutual interpenetration—*Durchdringung*—of the two opposite principles.

[3] (Our own translation.) "Geist und Drang, die beiden Attribute des Seins, sie sind, abgesehen von ihrer erst werdenden gegenseitigen Durchdringung – als Ziel –, aber auch in sich

This, then, is the statement of the real state of affairs in being itself. The result is that God himself emerges only in the spiritual acts of man. God must continue to realize himself (to become *real*) within the evolving vitalistic impulse of nature as spirit more and more transcends life by its own activity.

For us the basic relationship of man to the World-ground lies in this, that in man—who, as such, both as spirit and as organism is only a partial centralizing of the spirit and drive of the Being *per se*—I say, in man himself this World-ground directly comprehends and realizes itself.[1]

The original Being [*das Urseiende*] becomes conscious of itself in man in the same act by which man sees himself grounded in this being. We need but transform this thought, previously presented too intellectualistically, so that man's knowledge of being so grounded is the result of the active commitment of our being to the ideal demands of *deitas* and the attempt to fulfill this demand. In and through this fulfillment, man cooperates in the creation of God, who emerges from the Ground of Being in a process whereby spirit and drive interpenetrate increasingly.[2]

The final synthesis of man and being is achieved in the continuing spiritual evolution of God within the dynamics of the life-impulse.[3] Scheler concluded by appealing to man to have the courage to accept the fact of an "unfinished God." His appeal here carried with it the tone of Nietzsche's description of the Superman.

Scheler's metaphysics of man and of being is based upon his theory of man's place in nature and his understanding of spirit and person. This

nicht fertig; sie wachsen an sich selbst eben in diesen ihren Manifestationen in der Geschichte des Lebens der Welt." *Stellung*, 85; vf. *Man's Place*, 93–94. It is to be noted that Scheler consistently states that life and spirit are the two attributes *known to us*. He deliberately leaves open the possibility of further unknown attributes that may eventually evolve in spirit's (being's) more complete realization of itself. This parallels Spinoza's theory that extension and thought are the two essential attributes of Being known to us from among an infinity of such attributes.

  [1] (Our own translation.) "Für uns liegt das Grundverhältnis des Menschen zum Weltgrund darin, dass dieser Grund sich im Menschen – der als solcher sowohl als Geist – wie als Lebewesen nur je ein Teilzentrum des Geistes und Dranges des 'Durch-sich-Seienden' ist – ich sage: sich in Menschen selbst unmittelbar erfasst und verwirklicht." *Stellung*, 84; cf., *Man's Place*, 92.

  [2] *Man's Place*, 92–93. "Das Urseiende wird sich im Menschen seiner selbst inne in dem selben Akte, in dem der Mensch sich in ihm gegründet schaut. Wir müssen nur diesen bisher viel zu einseitig intellektualistisch vertretenen, Gedanken dahin umgestalten, dass dieses Sichgegründetwissen erst für die ideale Forderung der Deitas und des Versuches, sie zu vollstrecken, und in dieser Vollstreckung der aus dem Urgrunde werdenden 'Gott' als die steigende Durch-dringung von Geist und Drang allererst mitzuerzeugen." *Stellung*, 84. For Scheler, *Deitas* comprises the purely spiritual attributes of the highest Ground of Being. Cf. *Man's Place*, 70.

  [3] Ernst Cassirer has a very clear description of the problem of life and spirit in Max Scheler. E. Cassirer, "'Spirit' and 'Life' in Contemporary Philosophy." *The Philosophy of, Ernst Cassirer*, (Evanston, Illinois: The Library of Living Philosophers, Inc., 1949. (Vol. VI.) 857–880.

theory of being was meant to resolve the age-old tensions of realism-idealism, of the Dionysian and Apollonian elements in man, of the "natural" and the "humanistic" factors in culture, society and history. Scheler hoped that his "metaanthropological" theory of being would give a fitting climax to all scientific theories of evolution by allowing the evolution of life to develop into the self-realization of spirit within the Godhead itself. This theory of being remained the basis for Scheler's views on man, on nature, on sociology, on history and upon the forms of knowledge. It agreed well with his early views on person and, as we shall see, with his whole phenomenology of community. Man lives not only in community with other men, but man also lives in communion with all the levels of being.

CHAPTER THREE

MAN'S KNOWLEDGE OF MAN

Scheler felt strongly that a fresh, deliberate reconsideration of the whole problem concerning the knowledge of others must be made. Such a study must carefully study its own presuppositions, its metaphysical underpinnings and its practical applications. The problem is crucial in the history of human thought. With approval he quoted the words of Ernst Troeltsch:

> The main problem here is the question of our knowledge of other minds; for this is the peculiar presupposition of history, and in general a central issue for all philosophy, since the possibilities and difficulties of any common thought and philosophizing all depend upon it.[1]

The phenomenology of community must begin with the question of our knowledge of others.

Scheler himself arrived indirectly at the problem of man's knowledge of other men. It was in working out his theory of ethics that he discovered that he needed to expand his theory of sympathy; but sympathy, in turn, presupposed man's knowledge of other men. Therefore, Scheler's explicit discussion on mutuality and community in human knowledge occurred in his two editions of *The Nature of Sympathy*.[2]

The sequence of topics in the revised edition of *Sympathy* is quite disorganized. However, two very general directions of thought are constantly present. The first is a negative criticism against false theories

---

[1] As quoted in *Sympathy*, 1. "Im Mittelpunkt steht hier die Frage nach der Erkenntnis des Fremdseelischen, die die eigentliche Erkenntnistheorie der Geschichte ist, überhaupt ein Zentralpunkt aller Philosophie ist, weil auf ihr die Möglichkeiten und Schwierigkeiten gemeinsamen Denkens und Philosophierens überhaupt beruhen." M. Scheler, *Wesen und Formen der Sympathie* (Frankfurt/Main: G. Schulte-Bulmke, 1948) XIV. Much of Scheler's long preface to the second edition of *Sympathy* was to justify his decision to amplify the Appendix of the first edition ("On our ground for assuming the existence of other selves") into a new and independent part (Part Three) in the second edition. Part Three is entitled simply: "Other Minds" (*"Vom fremden Ich"*).

[2] The chief source for the present chapter is Scheler's major work on sympathy. Scheler had completed the first edition of *Sympathy* in 1912, but he published it simultaneously with *Formalism* in 1913. Cf. "Preface to the First Edition," *Sympathy*, 1. This study was to be the first of a projected series of studies tentatively entitled, "The Laws of Meaning within Emotional Life." The series itself was never actually realized by Scheler, Cf. Maria Scheler's introduction to the fifth edition: *Sympathie*, VI; *Sympathy*, xliv.

of sympathy. The second is a positive phenomenological exposition of the "essence and forms" of sympathy itself. The present chapter will emphasize the first of these two aspects. It will delineate the historical and critical background of Scheler's thought, as it touched upon the problems of sympathy and the perception of others. Then Scheler's own statement of the proper questions concerning the perception of others will be studied, along with his own solution to the problem. A subsequent chapter will take up the positive study of sympathy itself, as well as other particular modes by which men live together.

CRITICAL SURVEY ON THE NOTION OF SYMPATHY

In the introductory paragraph to the First Part of *Sympathy*, Scheler restated explicitly that it was primarily ethical considerations that prompted him to undertake a thorough study of sympathy. The ethical systems of the British moralists, Rousseau, Schopenhauer and Nietzsche rested upon particular theories of sympathy.[1] Scheler felt that his own theory of value-ethics must be able to rest upon a fundamental metaphysics and to supply a completely consistent and meaningful theory of how man lives together with other men.

Scheler consistently maintained his own positive definition of the essence of sympathy. He achieved this definition only through a carefully controlled phenomenological investigation of the sympathy phenomenon. The essence of sympathy includes two fundamental elements. First of all, the one who sympathizes with another must consciously perceive the emotional state of the other individual. Secondly, he must *feel* that same emotion, not necessarily in himself, but as emanating from the other. Therefore, the one who sympathizes, literally, "feels with" the other self; he participates in the emotional state of the other. As we shall see, Scheler employed these two basic elements of the essence of sympathy in his criticism of all past and present theories of sympathy.

A primary concern of Scheler was to distinguish his phenomenological investigations from all empirical psychological studies which he loosely labeled a "descriptive and genetic psychology." By this term he wanted to include the schools of associationist psychologists, biological evolutionists and the contemporary, scientific, experimental psychologists. Here he included all the men from Hume, Darwin and Spencer, to Wundt, Lipps, Bergson and Köhler. According to Scheler, all these

[1] *Sympathie*, 1; *Sympathy*, 3.

"psychologists" attempted to give a "genetic" description of man through an analysis of man's purely physical causal origins.[1] In the biological sciences, the causes of man and of his individual and group behavior were sought in man's physical, organic environment. In strictly psychological experimentation, the genetic scientific method artificially isolated various elements of a total psychological experience in order to *explain* the objective origin and causes of the composite experience. All the various genetic theories as grouped together by Scheler, attempted to describe the origin of man's feeling for his fellow-man along various lines of causal explanation.

Since the time of Hume, the associationist psychologists have artificially dissolved our unified experiences into isolated sense data which, in turn, must be reconstructed and synthesized in man's final perception of things. In such a case we would first know only the sensible, bodily characteristics of another man. By a second act, "the argument from analogy," we compare the bodily actions of our neighbor (which we perceive through external perception) with our own bodily reactions to our own interior psychic states (as perceived in inner perception). Finally, by an act of inference we conclude to the actual inner emotional state of the other. For example, we see an individual's face is tight and drawn; we know we look this way (by both outer and inner perception) when we are in pain; therefore, we infer that his bodily condition must be evidence of his own feeling of pain. It is to be noted that, up to this point, we would have gained only knowledge (apprehension) of the other's state: we have not *felt* his emotion, understood it, or responded to it in any way.

Scheler rejected the argument from analogy completely. It failed to consider phenomenologically what is genuinely and originally given in the unified human experience—"given in the sense of an original 'perception'" (*gegeben im Sinne originären "Wahrnehmens"*).[2] Only doctors and scientists, in a totally artificial situation, are permitted by their

---

[1] Ch. III of Part One, "Genetic Theories of Fellow-Feeling," is the longest extended treatment of this topic: *Sympathie*, 38–54; *Sympathy*, 37–50. Scheler can be justified in including these men and their systems in a single class of "genetic psychology" only by his own very broad understanding of "genetic-causal-explanations."

[2] The word *originär* is a key term in phenomenological analysis. What is *originär* in an experience is not only those elements that are immediately and directly seen upon our *first* reflection upon an experience. Further phenomenological investigation may be necessary, with careful acts of reduction and "bracketing," to unveil dimensions of meaning within the same experience. These deeper elements are intuited to be as equally "original" data within the first experience as are the simpler elements. This continuing analysis of the experience-act, to reveal within it all its levels of meaning, is the peculiar activity of phenomenology. The aim is not to discover the *causes* of the various elements in that act; nor is there any act of *inference* to anything outside of that act.

method to make the abstraction by which the body of the individual is accepted as the initial datum. Scheler's strong contention was that the body of another is never given in itself as a primary datum: what we experience is the total meaningful expression of the other. In the very blush of another we perceive his shame, in his laughter we perceive his joy. We perceive these inner emotional states of the other directly, and not by a mediate act of analogy and inference. In our perception of others, their bodies become, as it were, a "field of expression" (als Ausdrucksfeld), symbolical of the meaning immediately perceived by us. In other words, the elements of the experiencing act must be analyzed for their meaningful and symbolic relations, and not in terms of causal relations.[1] The method of phenomenology is sharply contrasted here with all genetic, scientific methods which seek to know the physical *origins* and the *causes* of things.

An alternate solution to the associationist starting point is that of "projective empathy" (*projektive Einfühlung*) or the "mimic (imitative) impulse" (*Nachahmungsimpulse*). Having sensibly perceived the bodily condition of another, through "mimicry" or "imitation" we automatically and spontaneously reproduce in ourselves the emotion portrayed on the bodily features of the other. We then "project" our feeling into the other in order to perceive and "to feel" his emotion.

This explanation (accredited to Lipps) was attacked by Scheler in the first place as being a circular argument. As a psychological explanation, the theory of projective empathy attempted to give the causal-temporal sequence of steps involved in the perception of, and the emotional response to, the emotional states of others. Scheler asked: how can we respond with the same quality of emotion which is in the other, unless we have actually perceived that very emotion in him beforehand? How can I "imitate" what I do not know? Scheler noted that while the analogical argument had at least some rational support, the argument from empathy proceeded on blind faith in the assumption

---

[1] *Sympathie*, 5–8; *Sympathy*, 9–11. Cf. p. 40, n. 2 immediately above for a preliminary description of the phenomenological method on his point. In the present context Scheler used both the terms *Ausdrucksfeld* and *Symbolbeziehung* to describe the original content of the phenomenological experience of others. *Symbol* must not be taken so that a second mental act is required to uncover its further meaning. Scheler himself added this footnote: "We might also say that it is not the mere relation of a 'sign' to the presence of 'something,' whereby the latter is subsequently inferred; rather it is the relation of a genuine original being of the sign itself [*die Beziehung eines echten ursprünglich 'Zeichenseins'*]." *Sympathy*, 10, n.; *Sympathie*, 6, n. A *Zeichensein* is taken as a pure sign, a formal sign. Its very being is to be "expressive" of meaning. Scheler stated that the perception of a sensible *thing* entailed the fact of the thing's inner and back side (a common phenomenological example). Also, then, the perception of another's bodily expression immediately entailed our knowledge of the inner emotional state of the other. This did not involve a separate mental movement from sign to thing signified.

that "my feeling" corresponds to the feeling of the other. This is a prime instance of a strictly circular argument. Scheler's criticism met the genetic explanation on its own ground and found it inadequate.

Scheler did admit the phenomenon of reproductive or imitative emotion as one type of emotional experience. The facts in this case are these: upon observing externally the emotional state of another self, e.g. in grief, we recall some of our own experiences *similar* to his. We use this occasion to remember our own past experiences. Already, then, at this point (contrary to the strict theory of projective empathy) we must have had a true perception of the actual emotional state of the other. But in the feeling-experience itself, we never transcend our own selves and our own experiences. We never reach out to feel the other self in his own individual situation. This is *not* a case of true sympathy. In fact, if this were the *total* experience, we would be unjustified in *projecting* the very existence of the other self. Aesthetic empathy is an example of reproduced emotion without accepting the actual existence of the other. In other words, with the case of aesthetic empathy we become emotionally involved with the situation of another, e.g. the plight of the heroine in a fictionalized account, but we do not project the actual existence of the other.

In many instances, empathy can supply the actual causal explanation for our emotional moods. But Scheler maintained his criticism against projective empathy. He denied that this theory can supply the basic and fundamental explanation for the very origin and fact of our knowledge of, and our emotional feeling for, the emotional state of another. Furthermore, underlying this whole discussion was Scheler's more general criticism against all scientific attempts to *explain* the causal factors of sympathy, instead of trying to *understand* its meaningful-expressive elements and to gain a proper insight into the true essence of sympathy as a *feeling*—a feeling *with* someone else.[1]

Another type of "genetic" theory for sympathy described our feeling-with another as being the result of self-reflection and comparison

---

[1] *Sympathie*, 7–8; 50–54; *Sympathy*, 10–11, 45–50. In all discussions, the terms "before," "prior," "subsequent," "dependence," etc. must always be taken strictly within each particular context. In some discussions, as here in the genetic explanation of the argument from analogy and from empathy, there is reference to a causal sequence in which there is an actual temporal sequence passing from a "before" to a "subsequent" state. Scheler's own statement of phenomenological laws also often refer to a "prior" condition, but in this case there is reference to a strictly *essential* dependence and relationship between concepts, e.g., the insight into the essence of the cube demands the "subsequent" insight into the backside of the three-dimensional figure.

(*Überlegung*).[1] "How would it be if this had happened to me?" Scheler ascribed this position to those psychologists and ethicians who follow Rousseau and the French Enlightenment thinkers in their theory of the natural egoism of man. Scheler's criticism of this view is that it remains totally egoistic. All references to the actual states of the other person are perceived by me only to the extent that I hypothetically delude myself with the illusion that I am the other individual.[2]

Another type of egoism is evidenced in the case where someone is affected with different emotional states through his contact with others. He is sad with the sad, happy with the happy. Scheler carefully pointed out that this is *not* necessarily a case of feeling *with* the other through genuine sympathy. In a case of true sympathy we actually perceive the objective emotional state of the other self, but there need not be an identical emotional response on our part.[3] Otherwise, the case is merely an isolated instance of "emotional infection."

By "emotional infection" (*Gefühlsansteckung*) Scheler referred to those phenomena by which emotional states become "contagious" to others. He cited the examples of giggling girls, of mourning women, of a party in a pub where newcomers are immediately infected with the prevailing atmosphere. The process of infection presupposes no knowledge of the cause or the origin of the emotional mood. It is an involuntary process and, as such, is irresponsible, which fact accounts for the violence of mobs. Darwin, Spencer and many positivists have mistaken this herd-consciousness in man as the result of some more basic social instinct and as the source of much of man's social nature, his ethos and his political institutions.[4] Scheler accepted the wealth of interesting factual, empirical details that Darwin and Spencer have contributed to our knowledge of the phylogenetic origin and extension of sympathy in man. But Scheler insisted that the phenomenon of "fellow-feeling" of true sympathy is itself primary and basic and irreducible to anything else.[5] Scheler would not admit that sympathy is a late epiphenomenon, consequent upon some "social instinct." All social life presupposes a prior fact of living *with* others.[6]

[1] Heath translates *Überlegung* in this context simply and exclusively as "comparison." In itself the word means "reflection," "deliberation."
[2] *Sympathie*, 41–42; *Sympathy*, 39–41.
[3] *Sympathie*, 42–43; *Sympathy*, 41–42.
[4] *Sympathie*, 11–15; *Sympathy*, 14–18.
[5] Cf. *infra*, Ch. IV, Section one, for a discussion on the use of terms for *sympathy*.
[6] Ch. VIII of Part One, "The Phylogenetic Origin and Extension of Fellow-Feeling," continues this discussion. *Sympathie*, 142–48; *Sympathy*, 130–34. This is one example of the lack of strict order in the work as a whole.

By emotional identification (*Einfühlung*) an individual is so infected with the situation in which he discovers someone else that the former identifies himself totally with the latter. This can be purely fictional and temporary, as in the case of a spectator watching an acrobat. This, then, in a case of empathy (*Einfühlung*) rather than of true identification. Or it can become permanent and incontrollable, as in severe cases of hysteria. Some primitives identify themselves with a totem, a hypnotist-subject is identified with the hypnotist, weak personalities may allow themselves to be identified with the whims and wishes of the strong. These are only a few of the many forms of emotional identification. The vain man (and men suffering from some forms of hysteria) lives only in the image he creates in the eyes of others: he becomes a spectator to himself in identifying himself with the onlooking public. Emotional identification is the complete reversal of the various forms of egoism, but it is just as vulnerable to criticism when it purports to explain the phenomenon of sympathy. I do not really know or sympathize with someone else, e.g., when I lose my own self-identity to a hypnotist, if I completely lose myself within the power of the other individual. True sympathy functions within the poles of two completely individual selves who, literally, "feel with" each other.[1]

Along with the criticism of genetic theories of sympathy, Scheler considered a group of theories he described as metaphysical. He thought that the metaphysical theories of sympathy were closer to the true understanding of sympathy than the genetic theories. His reasoning here is interesting.

At all events, metaphysical theories of fellow-feeling have a considerable advantage, in their approach to the problem, over empirical theories of the psychological and genetic type with which we have been dealing. They accept, in principle, what our analysis has confirmed and what our criticism and rejection of the empirico-genetic theories had reinforced from the other side, namely, that vicarious and companionate feelings are *basic phenomena*, which can only be *exhibited* as they actually are, without being derivable from more elementary facts on psycho-genetic lines. Irreducible elementary phenomena—in so far as their real existence [*Dasein*] is explicable at all—can be explained *only metaphysically*, i.e., in reference to the really existing [*real Seienden*] and to its order.[2]

[1] *Sympathie*, 15–38, 44–46; *Sympathy*, 18–36, 42–44.
[2] *Sympathy*, 55–56. (The last sentence is our own translation.) "Auf alle Fälle haben die metaphysischen Theorien des Mitgefühls schon in ihrer Fragestellung etwas Wichtiges vor den oben behandelten empirisch-psychologischen und – genetischen Theorien voraus. Sie sitzen prinzipiell als richtig eben das an, was auch unsere Analyse erwiesen und unsere Kritik und Ablehnung der empirisch-genetischen Theorien auf negativen Wege erhärtet haben: dass Nachfühlen und Mitgefühl *Urphänomen* sind, die nur in ihrem Wesen *aufgewiesen* werden können, nicht aber psychogenetisch aus einfacheren Tatsachen ableitbare Erscheinungen. Unableitbare Urphänomene aber sind – soweit ihr Dasein noch erklärbar ist – eben auch *nur metaphysik erklärbar*, d.h. mit Heranziehung desjenigen real Seienden und seiner Ordnung." *Sympathie*, 60.

Scheler himself deliberately avoided a systematic treatment of metaphysics in *Sympathy*. Such a discussion would have been out of place.
But there were constantly present the two underlying themes of life and
spirit (*die Metaphysik des organischen Lebens zusammen mit der Metaphysik
des Geistes*).[1] We shall see how these two principles function as the most
basic metaphysical ground of most of the subsequent discussion. It
should also be noted that the so-called "metaphysical" theories are
discussed in this work only to the extent that those theories are relevant
to the problem of sympathy.

Schopenhauer's theory of universal pity was of great interest to
Scheler both for its relevance to ethics and for its basis in a metaphysics
of will. Scheler praised Schopenhauer for his reintroduction of emotion
into ethics (against the bare formalism of Kant) and for his recognition
that in pity we commiserate immediately with others. Moreover,
Schopenhauer correctly grounded the phenomenon of pity in some
more basic unit of life. However, Scheler criticized Schopenhauer on
several points. Schopenhauer's metaphysics was a life-monism, identified as blind-will, and, as such, was subject to the general criticism
against all metaphysical monisms; this criticism will be developed
below. Furthermore, Schopenhauer falsely accepted fellow-suffering
(*Mitleid*) as the primary phenomenon, whereas for Scheler it was only a
special instance of a more general fellow-feeling (*Mitgefühl*). Also,
Schopenhauer falsely ascribed the principle of individuation between
men to their place in the space-time continuum. Finally, Schopenhauer's pessimism was evidence enough that his ethical theory based
on universal pity involved a fundamental subversion of values.[2]

Theories of metaphysical *monism* were of two types: the one held for a
unity of *organic life* among all things in the cosmos, the other held a
monism of *spirit* among spirits. Scheler rejected all forms of monism by
insisting that authentic fellow-feeling necessarily entailed a "distance"
between individuals and an explicit awareness of this separateness. The
argument here was based almost exclusively upon the proper phenomenological investigation of the phenomena of sympathy.

A monism of spirit arises from different forms of egocentrism, of
solipsism and of a universal consciousness. In every instance there is the
illusion that a person's subjective environment is the objective world
itself. For a "spiritual monist" others existed only to the extent that
they were a part of the subject's own consciousness: all reality was

---

[1] *Sympathie*, 59–60; *Sympathy*, 55.
[2] *Sympathie*, 54–59; *Sympathy*, 51–55.

reduced to its unified spiritualized idea. Scheler declared that such a view failed to grasp the full meaning of our "feeling with" another as with a distinct individualized mind. Our fellow-man is experienced as equal in worth, equal in reality to ourselves, but as *distinct* from ourselves. Full phenomenological investigation discovers ample evidence for the unique individuality of the other and for a realm of his absolute privacy, without destroying the intrinsic teleological relationship of mutual, social communication between ourselves and him.[1]

The monistic *metaphysics of life* defines sympathy in terms of emotional identification with some basic vital impulse. Thus, man's social nature was the effect of some instinctive drives (sexual, herd instinct, types of hypnotism), so that all men are enveloped in a single sphere of vital activity. Buddhist thinkers were included with Schopenhauer, Bergson and Simmel as leading proponents of this theory.[2]

Scheler defended what he considered a genuine Christian optimism about the goodness of life. St. Francis of Assisi served as an ideal for him. He opposed the optimism of Francis to the pessimism of Indian thinkers and of Schopenhauer who preached a mystical identification in suffering with the cosmos which is essentially evil.[3] Moreover, we have seen that at the organic level, Scheler recognized not only a simple monistic life impulse. He also defended the reality of the individually existing things. These he defined as distinct centers of vital activity, each with its own in-and-for-itself being. Such a doctrine was meant to resolve a pure organic monism by admitting a multiplicity of living things.

Actually, it was only later that Scheler worked out in better detail the main formulae by which he could speak meaningfully of the multiplicity of organic beings. However, the extact reality of this multiplicity of beings remained ambiguous. Scheler allowed no ontological principle, such as a substantial form or of some basic entelechy, to serve as the real, intrinsic principle unifying and centralizing the activities of living things. Living things are experienced as dynamically unified in field and function. Scheler's type of phe-

---

[1] *Sympathie*, 60–74; *Sympathy*, 56–68.

[2] *Sympathie*, 59–61; *Sympathy*, 56–57.

[3] Cf. chapter five of Part One, "The Sense of Unity with the Cosmos in Some Representative Temperaments of the Past." *Sympatjie*, 84–104; *Sympathy*, 77–95. Scheler discussed here the meaning of mysticism and vitalism in nature from the point of view of Christian faith. Underlying the whole discussion remain the basic unresolved metaphysical tensions between life and spirit.

nomenology could proceed no further in defining or explaining this unity.[1]

However, Scheler's chief criticism against a strict monism of organic life was that it also reduced all the phenomena of spirit to mere lower life processes. We have seen that Scheler repeatedly and vigorously stated that the full phenomenon of spirit cannot be reduced to a single, biological principle. Spirit, for Scheler, was not an accidental evolution, not a mere increase in quantitative perfection, not a "sublimation" of some lower life. Life and spirit were irreducible to each other. Moreover, within the realm of spirit itself, persons are immediately individualized in their original constitution. Thus, there is also multiplicity at the level of spirit.

In short, Scheler outlined two metaphysical theories of monism, the one holding for a monism of life, the other for a monism of spirit. Scheler resolved this situation by accepting both principles in a basic *metaphysical dualism* of life and spirit. Within each sphere there are individualized centers of vital and spiritual activity.

Scheler was left with the problem of the unity of man. How is man's person (the concrete center of spiritual acts) united to his vital center? Scheler's answer was elliptical but consistent. "No substantial *bond of unity* exists between spirit and life, *between spirit and life*, between person and life-center, but only a *dynamic causal bond of unity*."[2] "It is the same concrete, unified person to whom I know belong, both the *I* as well as the body (the animate as well as the inanimate body). The *I* as well as the body find its last individualization in its experienced state of belonging to a unified *person*."[3] Spirit is dependent upon and imbedded in the lower life processes. But the type of unity between an individualized spirit (person) and its concrete center of life activities is merely an experienced unity of dynamic relations.

---

[1] Cf. *Sympathie*, 84; *Sympathy*, 76. Scheler himself recognized this difficulty. In a footnote (n. 2) on this page in *Sympathy* he stated that he planned to publish soon a study on the system of the "unity of life" in which there would be combined the data of science (morphology) and phenomenology. This work was never published, although much of the material was included in *Man's Place*.

[2] (Our own translation.) "Kein substantiales, ein nur *dynamisch kausales Einheitsband* besteht uns *zwischen Geist und Leben*, Person und Lebenszentrum." *Sympathie*, 83. (Cf. *Sympathy*, 76.) The fact that Scheler introduced *causal* in this description is interesting. Perhaps he was hard pressed to discover a proper term which would describe the dynamic relations which exist here. However loose his use of this term, its introduction seems to indicate that he was casting around for a better formula and a better understanding of man's unity.

[3] (Our own translation.) "Da es dieselbe konkrete einheitliche Person ist, der ich Beides, das Ich und den Leib (als Seelen- und Körperleib), zugehörig weiss. Sowohl das Ich wie der Leib findet in der erlebbaren Zugehörigkeit zur einheitlichen *Person* seine letzte Individualisierung." *Sympathie*, 262; cf. *Sympathy*, 243.

QUESTIONS CONCERNING THE PERCEPTION OF OTHERS

Scheler's theory of sympathy presupposed the perception of others. Obviously, I cannot respond sympathetically to another without being aware that he is someone different from and outside of me. Scheler constructed his theory of sympathy on two fundamental principles. Both of these principles are basic to a full discussion on man's knowledge of man. 1) Persons are individualized in the very acts by which they are constituted persons, i.e., concrete centers of spiritual acts. 2) The actual perception of others is a fundamental experience, a primary given phenomenon, not reducible to anything else. We will briefly discuss these two principles as preliminary to our listing of Scheler's series of questions dealing with the problem of perceiving others.

The individuation of persons is a recurring theme in *Sympathy*. We have already seen that Scheler's theory of person and of the *I* demanded that the principle of individuation between persons could not reside in the body or in any space-time reference. These arguments are repeated at some length here.

If we abstract from the bodies of persons and from those differences of a spatio-temporal order, if we further abstract from everything which possibly distinguishes the content of their consciousness (from all possible levels of consciousness of both the inner and outer environmental world), even then, persons *differ* through their very own qualified being [*durch das Sosein ihrer selbst*] as concrete act centers. ... Indeed, they are the only examples of "independently existing beings" (substances) ["*selbstständigen Daseins*" (*Substanzen*)] which are individualized exclusively in themselves. Since persons cannot be individualized, like inorganic bodies which are otherwise identical in their qualified being, through space and time and through number and mass, because as pure act-centers persons transcend space and time (however much they may operate in the objective spatio-temporal world through the *mediation* of that life-force [*Lebenskraft*] in its construction of the body from dead matter, persons can and must be individualized through their own simple being [*durch ihr pures Sosein selbst*], through their own personal "essence." Inorganic bodies [*Körper*] and even men's bodies [*Leiber*] can be identical in their qualified being [*soseinidentisch*] and still be really different through their different positions in the spatio-temporal order. "Persons" are really distinct in the last instance only because they differ in their own qualified being [*soseinverschieden*], because they are *absolute* individuals. Schopenhauer's theory that the only *principium individuationis* is in the spatio-temporal order is therefore a completely false theory.[1]

---

[1] (Our own translation.) "Personen sind, auch wenn wir von ihren Leibern und deren Verschiedenheiten im Raumzeitsystem absehen, ferner absehen von allen, was ihren möglichen Bewusstseins*inhalt* (allen möglichen Bewusstseinssphären der Innen-Aussen-Mitwelt) in sich verschieden macht, immer noch durch das *Sosein ihrer selbst* als konkrete Aktzentren *verschieden*. ... Ja, sie sind die einzigen Fälle 'selbstständigen Daseins' (Substanzen), die ausschliesslich in sich individuiert sind. Gerade weil sie nicht durch Raum und Zeit, noch Zahl und Menge (bei sonstiger Identität des Soseins) individuiert sein können – wie Körper, z.B. –

This rather long passage is one of several explicit discussions on the problem of individuation.[1] We see here, first of all, the consistency of Scheler's doctrine on the philosophy of person with that of *Formalism*. *Person* was always defined as the concrete center of spiritual acts, which totally transcends the spatio-temporal world of matter. This consistency persists through *Sympathy* and throughout all his later works.

But our main point here is to study Scheler's methodological treatment of the problem. He seems satisfied to rest his case upon accepted principles and definitions. These, in turn, take on all the force of basic, irrefutable metaphysical principles. But as a matter of fact, these principles themselves are no stronger than the original arguments by which *they* were established. This involves the phenomenological investigation of the knowledge of ourselves and of our perception of others. Furthermore, since the core of the discussion centers around the problem of person, our study should transcend the body-self level by a series of reductions until we reach the level of transcendental psychology and study the phenomena of pure spirit and of pure person. The real validity and strength of Scheler's whole position depend upon a series of prior phenomenological studies, which he does not actually supply for us.

The second basic principle for Scheler was his position on *the actual, inner perception of others*. Between 1913 and 1923, he came to realize more forceably the crucial importance in his thought of the theory of the perception of other selves. That we know others is not just a social fact which we can explain according to its causal origins. It is a very meaningful phenomenon whose full understanding gives insight into a general metaphysics of man and of being.[2] For these reasons, Scheler felt it necessary to expand what was only an Appendix of *Sympathy* in 1913 into a whole new part, Part Three, in the second edition of *Sympathy* in 1923.

---

sondern als pure Aktzentren über Raum und Zeit erhaben sind (wie immer sie durch die *Vermittlung* der den Leib aus totem Material aufbauenden Lebenskraft in die objektive raumzeitliche Welt hineinwirken können), müssen und können sie nur durch ihr *pures Sosein selbst* (ihr personales 'Wesen') verschieden sein. Körper und auch noch Leiber können sosein-identisch sein und doch realiter verschieden durch ihre verschiedene Lage im Raumzeit-system. 'Personen' sind real verschieden in letzter Instanz nur, weil sie soseinverschieden, d.h. wel sie *absolute* Individuen sind. Die Lehre Schopenhauers, dass die raumzeitliche Ord-nung das einzige principium individuationis bilde, ist daher eine ganz irrige Lehre." *Sympathie*, 71; cf. *Sympathy*, 65. It might be noted that Scheler also criticized St. Thomas's use of the principle of individuation. Scheler recognized that his own definition of person was very similar to the scholastic definitions of separated soul and pure form.

[1] For other examples, see *Sympathie*, 82–83; 134–37; *Sympathy*, 75, 120, 122–23.

[2] Cf. his refreshing discussion of this problem in the openings pages of Part Three, esp. the last page, *Sympathie*, 228–31; *Sympathy*, 213–15. He calls the problem "a metaphysics of man's knowledge of man."

A detailed discussion of Part Three of *Sympathy* is essential for understanding Scheler's theory about man's knowledge of man. The discussion becomes difficult already at the level of language itself. From
our study of Scheler's meaning of Person and *I*, we have seen that these
terms take on a very technical meaning for Scheler. Since Schelerian
vocabulary has not yet been set in English, it is difficult to assess either
English translations or English studies until some definite consistency
in the use of terms is established.[1] Heath's translation of *Sympathy*, is
accurate enough on the whole, but it cannot be trusted fully within a
closely restricted study of very technical details.

The very title of Part Three is: "Vom fremden Ich." Heath translates
this: "Other Minds"; literally, it is: "Concerning the Alien *I*." Obviously, this whole discussion must be kept within the context of the
person and the *I*. Our own discussion will adhere as closely to Scheler's
terminology as is practicable in English. *Geist* will continue to be translated consistently as *spirit*, *Person* as *person*, *Ich* and all its derivatives
(*Ichheit*) as *I*, *Selbst* as the inner psychic *Self*, in contrast to the loose
reflective use of *self*, such as "hearing oneself talk." *Seele* and its derivatives will be translated as *anima* or *soul*, but as we shall see, this is a
particularly ambivalent term. In some discussions, to avoid any specifi-
cation about individual *persons* or other *I*'s, we will speak simply of
others or of *other individuals*.

The main purpose of Scheler's new discussion on the problem concerning the perception of others was to distinguish clearly the separate
questions involved in the problem, to put the questions in proper order
and, in this way, to work out their solutions systematically. Scheler
distinguished six separate questions.

1. Under the first question, Scheler made three short enigmatic
queries. Our own discussion will list these three questions and then
also supply Scheler's answers to the questions as given elsewhere within
the context of his thought.

---

[1] Perhaps the best studies on Scheler in English are those by Alfred Schutz. (Towards the
end of his life, Schutz dropped the *u*-umlaut in his name.) But Schutz was not always too
successful in his choice of English vocabulary. He consistently used "principally" as the
equivalent of the German *principiell*, which should mean, "in principle." But more to the
point here, Schutz chose to translate *Geist* as *Mind*. Thus he states: "Mind and its correlate,
Person, is principally not objectifiable." We would state: "Spirit and its correlate Person, is,
in principle, not objectifiable." A. Schutz, "Scheler's Theory of Intersubjectivity and the
General Thesis of the Alter Ego," *Philosophy and Phenomenological Research*, 2 (1941–42), 325.
We see from the title of this article, Schutz translates *Ich* as *Ego*. We prefer *I* to avoid con-
fusion with all psychological and psychoanalytic literature on the Ego. But with those very
minor reservations in respect to terminology, this long article is an excellent study on
Scheler's theory on the perception of others.

What essential relationship exists between *I* and community in general, both in the ontic sense and in our knowledge of essences?[1] Scheler immediately reworded this question by asking again: does there exist here an essential relationship of evident connection, or is this association always a merely factual and contingent one? Scheler's answer, of course, was that phenomenology has as its purpose to investigate the essential relationships between intuited essences. Does the full phenomenological investigation of the essence of the *I* entail its inclusion within a community? This question is to be strictly separated from all factual, historical questions about the real existence of some definite, contingent *I* or of some definite, contingent community.

Finally, Scheler asked here a third question, which has new implications. Do there exist different kinds of genuine essential connections between "men" as vital beings and between "men" as beings of spirit and reason, or is one of these two relations purely contingent? Scheler's answer here was that the full essence of man included not only his spiritual-reasonable nature, but also his vitalistic nature. Therefore, man must be essentially related to other men within the full dimensions of his being; this includes both the vitalistic and the spiritual levels of man.[2]

2. The second question dealt with the strictly epistemological questions concerning the criteria necessary to judge the actual reality of things. Two questions are pertinent to the immediate discussion: How do I (the writer of these lines) know that a particular, definite community really exists? How do I judge that any definite alien *I* really exists? It is evident that, while these questions depend upon a previous total epistemology, yet each question must be answered with great care.

Scheler further sub-distinguished three questions of epistemology. a) What is the general reality-moment for an object (*Gegenstand*) and how is it given in an essential way to a spiritual subject?[3] Scheler's answer here as given consistently in all his works was that the fact of "resistance to objectification" is the criterion for reality. Only spirit can objectify such pockets of resistance into ideal essences. b) What is the mark of the *psychic* or *spiritual* reality of a conscious *I*, either of my own *I*

---

[1] "Ontic" here is the German word *ontisch*. Both Heath and Schutz translate it as "ontological." We prefer *ontic*, since its reference is to the concrete, real existence.

[2] *Sympathie*, 231–32; *Sympathy*, 216.

[3] Heath translates *geistiges Subjekt*—spiritual subject—as "conscious subject," a poor choice of terms, for it loses the strict distinction between person and lower forms of consciousness. Cf. *Sympathy*, 232.

or of an alien *I*, in contrast to the mere consciousness "of" this reality? How is this reality given?[1] This question, then, is directly involved in the problem of man's knowledge of man. c) In what way and by what means is the reality of an alien animate-spiritual center (*Realität eines seelisch-geistiges Zentrums*) originally given, over and beyond the mere knowledge of an alien conscious *I* and its content?[2] As we have seen, strict spiritual acts and persons (who are the unified centers of acts) cannot be objectified into knowledge. Therefore, the criterion concerning the reality of other persons must be had through some other means.[3]

3. The third question inquired into the origin of social consciousness. This discussion, for Scheler, was not a question about the empirical facts surrounding a child's temporal advancement to an explicit knowledge of others. Scheler here sought the phenomenological order of dependence between essential insights. His questions dealt with the foundation (*Fundierung*) for the various cognitive intentions at the level of transcendental psychology. The order of dependence and all references to a *before* and an *after* are made within the strictly essential order; they do *not* refer to an actual, temporal sequence as such.

For example, does knowledge of an alien *I* generally presuppose an acquired consciousness of one's own *I*? Scheler replied: yes. Does such knowledge originally presuppose a consciousness of the Self? Scheler replied: no. Does knowledge of an alien *I* presuppose a consciousness of God? Scheler replied: yes. Does knowledge of others presuppose a knowledge of nature and a knowledge of the reality of the outer world or is there an opposite dependence? Scheler made further distinctions at this point. Given the general universal condition that there is given to our consciousness "ideal meanings of signs," then our knowledge of an alien *I* in its activity as a spiritual subject is immediate and direct and presupposes nothing else. However, if reference is made to the vital, animate life of human subjects, there must be presupposed the whole area of expressive meaningfulness of living things in general.

---

[1] In this passage, Heath translates *psychisch* as "mental" and *Bewusstseinich* as a "conscious self" and *Selbstbewusstsein* as "self-*consciousness*." If one reads only his translation, the ambiguity of these terms is intensified.

[2] As we have noted, Scheler's use of *Seele* is difficult to assess. Does it mean *anima* does it mean *mind*, referring to mental operations, or does it mean *soul*? The word *psychisch* is just as ambiguous. For example, we have seen that in *Man's Place* where Scheler discusses the basic vital functions of plant life, *seelisch* and *psychisch* are used interchangeably to refer to Aristotle's meaning of *psyche* as the most basic life-principle. In some passages of *Formalism* and *Sympathy* this use of terms is present. In other contexts, the terms take on wider meanings. Each context must be studied carefully. After this, we will make no more detailed criticism of Heath's translation of terms. Our point has been made that the German must be consulted for a precise understanding of Scheler's meaning in each context.

[3] *Sympathie*, 232–33; *Sympathy*, 216–17.

Scheler insisted that originally (e.g. children and primitives) we perceive all of nature as *living*, and only subsequently can we distinguish the non-living from the living. Finally, Scheler asked, is our knowledge of the alien *I* before, simultaneous with, or subsequent to our knowledge of him as an organic form, as a living body within an environmental world? He answered: this knowledge is simultaneous.

These answers gave Scheler a preliminary outline according to which he worked out his detailed theories about man's knowledge of man and the forms by which man lives in community and society. His study was a purely philosophical study, as only phenomenology could be. Its investigations dealt only with pure essences (the essence of the *I* and the *I*'s relatedness to community). His final theory was elevated above purely contingent, historical conditions, even above the provincial conditions and attitudes of Western civilization. Such a phenomenological investigation of the universal essential social laws of man-living-in-community is sharply contrasted with both empirical-explanatory psychology and with socio-historical psychology. In this sense, Scheler described his study as a "transcendental psychology."[1]

4. The fourth series of questions discussed the competence and relevance of empirical psychology for the problem concerning man's knowledge of man. For all the value of empirical data, scientific psychology contributes very little to the philosophical issues at hand. Science presumes without investigation the very answers which philosophy seeks to know. Such truths include the real existence of fellow-men, the real flow of experiences in a temporal sequence, the retention of experiences in memory and the actual communication between men at many different levels. A transcendental psychology, according to Scheler's method of phenomenology, must hold in suspension all these facts until they become verified at some post-reductive level.

Scientific psychology must objectify its objects of study. Since person and its spiritual acts are non-objectifiable, they fall outside of the competence of science. Scheler rejected the formula by which thinking, willing, etc., are called "higher functions." These activities are *spiritual* acts, essentially transcending the level of mere functions.

Everything which can be accessible to experimentation lies exclusively in the limits of *vital-psychic* being and becoming, which has its own automatic, intrinsic teleology, that is, *below* the realm of 'free' spiritual acts of the person.[2]

[1] *Sympathie*, 233–37; *Sympathy*, 217–20.
[2] (Our own translation.) "Alles, was experimentell zugänglich sein kann, liegt ausschliesslich in den Grenzen des *vitalpsychischen* zielmässig automatischen Seins und Geschehens, d.h. *unterhalb* des Reiches der 'freien' geistischen Personakte." *Sympathie*, 240; cf. *Sympathy*, 223.

The spiritual person as such is intrinsically incapable of being treated as an object. The question then remains: how can one person in any way *know* or *get inside* another person? This is Scheler's key point in the whole discussion. His answer is that persons actually do communicate with one another through a participation in the being of another (*Seins-teilnahme*). Such participation presupposes the fact that a particular person is free to decide whether he will make himself available to the other person or not. Persons can be silent; they can actively conceal their inner being.

What is the nature of this participation in the spiritual acts of other persons? Very definitely, it is *not* knowledge in the ordinary meaning of the word, as being objectified or in any way accessible through experimental scientific psychology. A participates in the spiritual acts of B by co-performing those same acts with B, by re-living and re-executing B's personal acts. Therefore, A can make will-acts along with B; A can "feel with," or "sympathize with," B; A can subsequently re-live in thought and feeling other personal acts of B. Scheler's description of this active participation between persons was a key doctrine of *Formalism*.[1] This theory was basic to his theory of man's relation to others in person-community and to his philosophy of religion in describing man's relationship to God.[2] His phenomenological method was especially helpful in devising this theory of participation. This theory remains one of Scheler's most important contributions to contemporary thought.

5. The fifth question demanded the proper metaphysical orientation of the whole discussion. The theory of man's knowledge of man must be consistent with a definite type of metaphysics and epistemology. Thus, the theory of analogy fits within one type of metaphysics; a metaphysics of monism or of idealism will have other theories. Scheler demanded a logical consistency in each case, between metaphysics, the solution of the mind-body problem, and the problem of knowing other men.

Scheler, therefore, called for the proper ordering of the questions according to his own method of phenomenological insights into pure essences. He wanted to know, prescinding from all actual existence, the

---

[1] Cf. *supra*, Ch. II, section three.

[2] *Sympathie*, 237–42; *Sympathy*, 221–25. In a footnote he adds: "If God is thought of as a Person, it is equally inconceivable that there should be objective knowledge of Him; it is only by a *cogitare, velle, amare in Deo*, i.e., by a reliving of the divine life and the reception of His word, through which He first reveals His existence as a Person, that such knowledge is obtained." *Sympathy*, 224; *Sympathie*, 241.

essential relationship between the *I* and community in general. He demanded the critical justification of our knowledge of others within the context of our whole natural *Weltanschauung*.[1]

6. The last question sought the relationship between our knowledge of others and the question of moral values. Scheler denied that all ethical values depended exclusively upon our social duty to others. An absolutely single individual could still respond to some authentic moral values. On the other hand, person itself is given to us in the first instance as a *value*, and only subsequently, as an individually qualified being (*Sosein*). Further, such moral acts as love, responsibility, duty, gratitude, have a necessary reference to the existence of other persons— to other persons within community, bound together through moral solidarity. Intrinsic to this co-union of finite persons with one another is their relation with the Person of Persons, God. These are strictly dimensions of persons. This discussion leads immediately into the heart of the question about the basic social nature of man.[2] Our own discussion of this matter will appear in the chapter in our study of man in community.

THE PERCEPTION OF OTHERS

Scheler's purpose in distinguishing the above six questions was to establish the proper order of the questions and to treat their solutions in a systematic way. Accordingly, in the second chapter of Part Three of *Sympathy*, he proceeded to place the whole discussion in a very general context by defining the most general evidence of our experience of another.[3] According to the strict requirements of the phenomenological method, this was not an empirical or historical study of the causal origin of our knowledge of others. Scheler's study dealt only with the order and inner-relatedness of the essential insights into our social experiences and our social consciousness.

Chapter two is a short chapter which discusses only the most general background for defining the proper evidence for an alien *I*, a *Thou*. These pages are quite confused, because of the many elliptical references to and criticisms of, other positions. The more positive exposition of Scheler's own position was made in chapter three, "The Perception of Others."[4]

---

[1] *Sympathie*, 242–44; *Sympathy*, 225–27.
[2] *Sympathie*, 244–51; *Sympathy*, 221–33.
[3] Chapter two is entitled, "The General Evidence for the 'Thou,'" (*Die Du-Evidenz überhaupt*), *Sympathie*, 252–55; *Sympathy*, 234–37.
[4] The title is "Die Fremdwahrnehmung." Heath translates it as: "The Perception of Other Minds."

Scheler repeated here in the 1923 edition of *Sympathy* the example of Robinson Crusoe from *Formalism*. This time, however, he added some critical comments to clarify the exact meaning of his example. Scheler's Crusoe was neither the Crusoe of Defoe nor any actual historical person. For Scheler, Crusoe awoke on his desert island, mature and rational, but physically alone and completely unconscious of any past life with other people. This epistemologically described Crusoe had absolutely no empirical acquaintance with, no evidence of, any kind of an actual individual man—no footprints—with whom he could say: "We are in community !" Would such a Crusoe still be a social animal, a community being?

Scheler declared emphatically and consistently that a radical solipsist is impossible. His Crusoe would not say: "I am alone in the world; there is no community." Rather, he would say: "I know there is a community, I know I belong to one, but I haven't yet discovered empirically any individuals who make up the community." What is the source of such knowledge?

Scheler denied that any knowledge is innate: all knowledge is derived from experience. But knowledge need not be purely sensistic and factual, as the empiricists maintain. Scheler's Crusoe would experience within the dimensions of his being a sense of loneliness and a feeling of emptiness towards others. His emotional acts, such as love and sympathy, would remain unfulfilled, without a social response from an actual other being. Therefore, because of the emptiness within the intentionality of his performance-acts, this Crusoe would gain certain, objective, *a priori* and intuitional evidence (in the strict phenomenological meaning of all these terms) for the existence of some general Thou, evidence for some general community.

Phenomenology is the investigation of pure essences. Concrete examples for clear exposition are difficult to discover. Scheler's use of Robinson Crusoe is a valuable example, if it is used carefully. Knowledge is derived from experience (*Erlebnis*) but not from empirical data (*Erfahrung*). As much as possible, the body-world-environment is abstracted away. Intuition into an essence is possible even when beginning from an "empty" experience. Subsequent essential relations are then immediately subjoined to the primary essences.

Employing this method, Scheler made his conclusions. Man essentially possesses social feelings; an ever-present element of man's consciousness is a reference to community. This is man's most general evidence for the existence of a Thou in community.

We say (in our terminology) nothing else than that the world of the Thou or the world of community is an *independent essential sphere* of being, like the outer sphere, the inner world sphere, the body-environmental world sphere, the sphere of the divine.[1]

The world of the Thou and of community is irreducible to any other order of being.[2]

The primacy of the consciousness concerning others as an original datum of our experience was the single most important item for Scheler to establish. Therefore, he marshalled together all the arguments he could find.[3] Throughout this discussion he was still engaged in the refutation of the two alternate theories proposed to explain our perception of others: the analogical argument and the argument of projected empathy. His critique in this place, however, was a more carefully controlled phenomenological study of the whole problem.

At the lowest level, Scheler appealed to the data of comparative psychology to demonstrate that animals as well as men have an original, natural awareness of others. Apes respond automatically to group situations. Scheler also accepted the data of child psychology as evidence for his own position. A child apprehends various emotional states in others, such as "friendliness" or "unfriendliness." This is an immediate apprehension, directly intuited in the "expression" of those around the child: there is no question here of an analogical reference. Finally, children and primitives originally perceive all things to be living; only subsequently do they distinguish dead things from living things. However, the theory of projective empathy would have us believe that first there is a sensible perception of things as dead, and, only then, do we empathetically project our own sense of livingness upon the dead world. On the other hand, at the level of the *I*, a mere projection of the consciousness of my own *I* would not in itself give concrete knowledge of the alien *I* as other.

The two alternate solutions to the problem of perceiving others accepted two presuppositions. 1) Each presumed that one's own *I* is the primary datum of experience. 2) Each presumed that the *body* of the other, the appearance (*Erscheinung*) of his body, was the first datum in

---

[1] (Our Own translation.) "Wir sagen (in unserer Terminologie) nichts Anderes, als dass die Duwelt oder die Gemeinschaftswelt genau so eine *selbstständige Wesensphäre* des Seienden ist wie die Aussenweltsphäre, die Innenweltsphäre, die Leib-Umweltspäre, die Sphäre des Göttlichen. *Sympathie*, 254; cf. *Sympathy*, 236.

[2] A comparison of this sketch of the various spheres of being as given here in the 1923 edition of *Sympathy* agrees in substance with the many discussions in *Formalism*. Cf. esp., *Formalismus*, 162–63, n. 1.

[3] This is the bulk of the discussion in chapter three, *Sympathie*, 256–87; *Sympathy*, 238–64.

our experience of others. These two truths were accepted as self-evident, but Scheler examined both and rejected both.[1]

Is it phenomenologically accurate to say that it is one's own *I* that is first given in experience? As a matter of fact, we can think the thoughts of another, we can feel his feelings in the act of genuine sympathy. It sometimes is a separate task for us to distinguish our *own* thoughts, our own feelings, our own will, from the entire world of thought surrounding us. At this point, Scheler reversed completely the starting points from which the other two arguments began.

Scheler declared that what is immediately given in the human experience is a stream of conscious experiences at first undifferentiated between *I* and Thou. What is first experienced is the general sphere of the "we." To be sure, every experience ultimately pertains to an individual *I*. But it is only a late discovery within the emerging experience that fully determines for us whether a particular experience belongs to my *I* or to an alien *I* or is one that is shared mutually between us. It is in this sense that children and primitives at first tend to identify themselves with others. Only as a late phenomenon can they isolate themselves and identify their own Selves as individuals separate from the rest of the family community. In man's most primitive state of consciousness he lives "in" other people's experiences, rather than in his own.

Another consideration Scheler employed in his argumentation involved the distinction between *outer* and *inner* perception. The distinction here was not so much in respect to the subjective organs of perception, but in reference to the level of penetration into the object perceived. An outer perception of myself supplies a knowledge only of my external, bodily features; I touch myself, I see myself in a mirror, I hear myself talk. An inner perception achieves the awareness of the inner conscious states, of either my own Self or the Self of another. Animals can convey emotional states to one another, such as fear, without having an awareness of the center of consciousness, the Self itself. Men can know themselves and one another in a more intimate and interior way.

Does an act of external perception—of the body—necessarily precede (both in time and in essential dependence) the act of inner perception? An affirmative answer was the second self-evident assumption of the analogy and the empathy arguments. Scheler's examination of

---

[1] *Sympathie*, 263; *Sympathy*, 244. The examination of these two presuppositions take up the last pages of the book.

this presupposition led him to reject it also. The question is: can I have an inner perception of the alien *I*? I see a man smiling with joy. Do I "feel his joy," only by first "feeling you within me" and then ascribing "joy-feeling" to him? In this case, inner perception is possible only within me. All analogous conclusions and empathetic projections in respect to an alien *I* are, for Scheler, fictions and delusions.

To establish his point that we have direct, immediate perception into the inner state of the alien *I*, Scheler proposed two counter arguments. The first argument was the continuation of his phenomenological description of man's primary experience. As we have just seen, Scheler maintained that man is first immersed in a stream of consciousness undifferentiated into an alien *I* and his own *I*. The primary given is a general consciousness of a "we." The perception of one's own Self is the most difficult of achievements—surely not the first.

Secondly, and more to the immediate point, there was Scheler's own phenomenological description of the body of the other. The other's body is a "field of expression" immediately intuited to reveal the inner psychic state of the other. It was in this context that Scheler repeated the former examples: in the blush we immediately perceive the shame of the other, in his smile, friendliness, in his folded hands, a plea for mercy. A child responds to the warm love and friendliness of its mother long before its sense of sight is developed to the degree that it can distinguish colors, patterns and faces in the environmental world.

Scheler's prime principle was that we do perceive other people's experiences by inner perception. Everyone can apprehend the experiences of his fellow-men just as directly (or indirectly) as he can his own. Obviously, the body-perception is the condition under which our inner perception takes place, but neither my body nor the other's perceived body actually controls the total content of the experience itself. An experience must be accepted in its totality, within which there are external, sensible elements, as well as direct perception of the other's inner state. For example, I do see the smiling face of the other as I perceive his joy. However, the complete meaningfulness of the total experience must not be reduced to the purely sensibly perceived elements.

Two final points should be kept in mind. By the "perception of others" Scheler did not restrict the discussion to mere *cognitive* awareness of others. There is a more basic and genuine perception of others also at the level of the emotions. Thus, we "feel with" others, or respond affectively to the emotional states of the other, and we feel a moral responsibility for the value of others. Secondly, this whole discussion must be related to Scheler's theory of the person. The bulk of the present discussion concerns the relationship of body-*I* to life community, the body-soul-essence of man, in his relation to other men. Therefore, this is the sphere of the *I* and the Thou, where, within the outer world of the *I*, there is the sphere of life community.

Scheler's theory of person remained outside this discussion, but is closely connected to it. Person and its acts cannot be objectified in knowledge; in this sense, alien *persons* are not directly perceived. However, while the alien person stands outside of and beyond the functions of his body-*I* (in Scheler's special meaning of function), it is precisely his person that is dynamically connected in field and function to his own body-*I*. We *can* participate in the being of the other person by co-achieving, pre-performing and re-executing our own spiritual acts along side those of the alien person in person-community.

It is only the person beyond the body-*I* who can reflect upon his own functions and objects to discover there the center of his inner consciousness. This center is his own Self. This is the strict description of man's unique prerogative in possessing "Self consciousness." Animals are conscious, but they are not conscious of their Self. The person does not reflect directly upon his own person, but upon his *I* or Self. In this sense, the *I* is always an object and never the subject of perception.

Many difficulties remain in trying to resolve the full meaning of Scheler's full doctrine. The distinctions between "acts" and "functions" is hard to maintain. While the *I* is defined as always an object, language itself will hardly permit this use. Scheler was carefully employing a type of phenomenological reduction, when he attempted to perform a complete analysis of the essence of the *I*. No reduction could ever isolate the person itself. Acts continue to emanate from the person—almost all the activities under discussion, perception, sympathy, love, etc., are, in source, spiritual acts of the person—but the person itself remains inaccessible. It is as if we have rays of light from a star which is outside our realm of observation. In this way, the ethical integrity of the person was preserved and the person of God (Who has no *I*, no Thou, no community) was preserved in His essential dignity. However, the understanding of the unity and the meaning of man remained more difficult than ever.[1]

---

[1] Husserl re-examined the problem of the knowledge of others in *Cartesianische Meditationen und Pariser Vorträge* (Haag: Martinus Nijhoff, 1950) Husserliana, Band I. *Cartesian Meditations: An Introduction to Phenomenology*. Translated by Dorion Cairns. (The Hague: Martinus Nijhoff, 1960). This work was an elaboration of two lectures which Husserl

Scheler's theory of man in society, of man in community and on the social forms of knowledge are little more than detailed applications of these basic principles on the meaning of person and *I* in his philosophy of man.

delivered at the Sorbonne in February of 1929. It does not seem to be accidental that Husserl made no public study of the problem of intersubjectivity until after the death of Scheler. In these lectures of 1929, however, (especially in the Fifth Meditation), it is evident how radically different in spirit and method was Husserl's treatment of the problem from Scheler's. Husserl contained the discussion at the level of strict transcendental phenomenology and allowed its solution only within the context of a post-reductive transcendental ego re-establishing contact with the objective world.

CHAPTER FOUR

MAN AND SOCIETY

For Scheler, the line between philosophical anthropology and sociology was very thin. Since man is other-oriented in his most original experiences, since man is social prior to being individual, the study of man necessarily and intrinsically includes the study of the social nature of man. Furthermore, both anthropology and sociology must be renovated according to the phenomenological criteria demanded for all strict sciences.

SOCIOLOGY

The pioneering spirit of Scheler was especially evident in those works he titled "Problems ... ." The major part of *Eternal* dealt with "problems" in the philosophy of religion; the major part of *Forms of Knowledge* was titled "Problems of a Sociology of Knowledge." These works were written through the years 1920 to 1923 and they reflected the instability and transitional character of his thought during these years.

Scheler's opening lines of *Forms of Knowledge* announced his purpose in writing this book. Primarily, he wanted to show that a sociology of knowledge was a unified part of the sociology of culture (*Kultursoziologie*). Within this context he wanted to show the systematic ordering of the various problems and the general direction that their solution would take. Perhaps the most important contribution Scheler offered was to demonstrate the relationship of the sociology of knowledge with all the other social, humane and scientific disciplines. He disclaimed all attempts at actually solving the individual problems themselves.[1]

Sociology was defined by Scheler as possessing two essential characteristics. As a science, sociology is not concerned with individual facts and events occurring in time. Such a study would be *history*. Sociology deals with universal rules, types and laws of man's social life according

---

[1] As we shall see, Scheler accepted much sociological theory from Comte, Tönnies and Durkheim, was responsive to Simmel and Weber in his own day, and was, in turn, an influence upon Mannheim.

to some average or logical ideal types. On the other hand, sociology is not a normative science, either in a moral sense or in the sense of setting up some ideal social order. Sociology merely analyzes and describes the predominant objective and subjective social activities of man in respect to the purely factual data of the case (*nach seinen tatsächlichen Formen*).[1] In other words, both of these formal elements maintain that the science of sociology must correspond to the strict phenomenological criteria demanded for all the sciences.

Scheler distinguished between *cultural sociology* (*Kultursoziologie*) and *realistic sociology* (*Realsoziologie*). This distinction was fundamental for Scheler and persisted consistently in all his social thought. The distinction was grounded in Scheler's metaphysical dualism of *spirit* and *life*. Its application to the many areas of anthropology and sociology is another instance of a radical unity in Scheler's thought as a whole.

All the elements of civilization which are exclusively reducible to the peculiar genius of man are elements derived from *spirit* in man. Thus, language, law, the arts—all the elements which set man's social life above the animals—all the elements which make up civilization or culture as such are studied by *cultural sociology*. These elements are called *ideal factors* (*Idealfaktoren*). On the other hand, the components of civilization which are reducible to the purely physical and natural elements are derived from *life*. These include all the geographical factors, such as climate and local natural resources, as well as all biological factors, such as evolution and instinctive drives. These elements comprise the *real factors* (*Realfaktoren*) of civilization. The three chief groups of real factors are blood, power and hunger. Their study is taken up by *realistic sociology*.

The ideal factors make up the superstructure (*Überbau*) of civilization; the real factors make up the substructure (*Unterbau*) of civilization. These are the two poles within which man has actually constructed a particular civilization in a particular historical time and place. It is within the province of sociology to study the essential and universal laws of the ordering of effective reality (*das Gesetz der Ordnung der Wirksamkeit*) between these ideal and real factors.[2]

We can understand Scheler when he declared that this fundamental distinction between ideal and real factors in civilization was not just a methodological division: this distinction had its roots sunk deep in

---

[1] *Wissensformen*, 17.
[2] *Ibid.*, 18–20.

Scheler's whole metaphysics and anthropology.[1] Just as spirit (*Geist*)
and the most basic impulse of life (*Drang*) are unified as attributes of
being itself, so also both the ideal and real factors are combined into a
single civilization. Spirit of itself is originally lacking all energy and all
drive; analogously, the purely rational ideas of logic, of law and of
religion, with all their projected ends (*Zwecke*), will never construct a
civilization. These are the empty dreams of Utopia; by themselves,
they form the facade of dandyism. On the other hand, the purely
natural factors, without the restraint and guidance of spirit, will lead to
utter chaos.

Spirit's control over life is twofold: The first control is negative in
character. This is the activity of restraint, of inhibition, of repression
(*Lenkung*). The second control is positive in character. Through ideas
and values, spirit positively guides and directs (*Leitung*) the impulsive
drives of life. The actual realization of such ideas is brought about only
to the extent that they are incorporated within the real order of life
processes.[2] Thus, again, the final reality of things is brought about
through the mutual interplay of spirit and life, of ideal and real factors.

In describing the mutual interaction of spirit and life as component
factors of civilization, Scheler possessed a functional schema to discuss
other philosophies of civilization and of history. Hegel's idealism was
criticized for accepting only the ideal factors of history without admitting that these ideas are realized only in the dynamic energy of real
factors. On the other hand, all naturalistic and deterministic theories of
history were criticized for failing to see the restrictive and directional
control which spirit in man imposes upon the purely natural factors in
his environment.

Among the naturalistic theories was Comte's sociology. Scheler accepted many terms and categories from Comte. Thus, the ideal superstructure of civilization was compared to Comte's notion of *liberté
modifiable*. The real substructure of civilization was related to Comte's
fatalité modifiable. Scheler accepted the notion that social laws were
composed of static and dynamic elements. The basic categories of
Comte's three stages of human progress—the religious, the meta-

---

[1] *Ibid.*, 20. In the Foreword to *Wissensformen*, Scheler declared in italics: "You can understand the metaphysics of the author only if you have read this book!"

[2] *Ibid.*, 21–23; *cf.* also *Man's Place*, 62, 68–69; *Stellung*, 57–58, 63. In a footnote on another
page of *Wissensformen* (p. 40) Scheler explained further: "Direction [*Leitung*] is the primary
function of spirit, restraint [*Lenkung*] is the secondary function. Direction is *the holding up of an
idea of value*, restraint is the *repression and non-repression* [*Hemmung und Enthemmung*] *of the instinctive impulse*, whose ordered motions realize the ideas. Direction conditions the kind of
restraint."

physical, the sociological—were accepted by Scheler. However, Scheler denied that these were temporal stages of successive development. Scheler accepted these three categories as three separate, irreducible, but simultaneous classes of human experience. Every man in the various dimensions of his being is at all times a religious, a philosophical and a social being.[1]

Within this context, Scheler defined two general laws to describe the possible types of interaction between the ideal and the real factors of civilization. The first law admitted the necessary interaction between the two classes of factors and then described the precise character which each type of factor contributed to the final full reality of a civilization. The actual existence (*Dasein*) of a civilization is a result of real factors; the qualified condition of that civilization (its *Sosein*) is the result of ideal factors. Spirit is the *determining* factor of civilization; natural causes and factors such as blood, power and economic factors, are the *realization* factors of a civilization. The examples used were those of Raphael, who needed his paint and brush in order to realize his imaginative figures in real art, and of Luther, who needed the cooperation of the German princes to spread his theory of "faith alone."

The second general law described the various types of relations that exist between all the factors of civilization. 1. The *ideal* factors are related to one another as static and dynamic, so that each concrete civilization exists in a third state which is a particular stratified arrangement of static and dynamic ideal factors. 2. The *real* factors are also related to one another as static and dynamic and as concretely existing in a particular combination. 3. Finally, the three modes of relationship both within the class of ideal factors and within the class of real factors are transcendentally related to one another in so far as the two classes of factors mutually interpenetrate each other.[2]

Admittedly, these laws satisfy the requirements of being universal and necessary, but they are so general that in themselves they are practically useless for detailed application in sociology. Scheler, however, felt that with these laws he could criticize most past theories of civilization by dividing them into "idealistic" and "naturalistic" theories. At the same time, he could sift through the many facts of history to isolate particular instances which exemplified the universal truth of what he called a "sociological fact" (*soziologische Tatsache*).

---

[1] *Wissensformen*, 23; cf. the essay "Über die positivistische Geschichtsphilosophie des Wissens (Dreistadiengesetz)," *Soziologie*, 27–35.
[2] *Wissensformen*, 22–23.

Within this discussion, he explained in more detail the three chief types of real factors: blood, power and economy (hunger). From one point of view, these three factors represent a temporal development in civilization: from tribal associations, to political states, to economic control. From another point of view, each factor is the social counter-part of individual human drives: blood and tribal relations are the fulfillment of the sex drive, political organizations fulfill man's drive for power, economic organizations supply man's need for food.

In every case, the spiritual-personal nature of man can restrain and direct the real factors of history to determine them according to strictly ideal concepts and values. The value of a particular civilization is judged by the order of values preferred in that civilization. By this principle, Scheler could criticize Marxism, economic liberalism and pure "power politics," because these theories chose a lower grade of values over the higher spiritual values of art, religion and ethics.[1]

From this brief description we see that Scheler had a very strict theory of sociology. It was closely connected with his theory of man and of metaphysics. At the same time, he was able to apply it to many detailed problems of history and of civilization.

In *Forms of Knowledge* and *Sociology*, Scheler accepted many truths discussed at length elsewhere in his writings. He called these truths *axioms* and accepted them without new discussion. One of the most basic axioms dealt with the various universal social forms in which men live together. This had been discussed in some detail in *Formalism* and formed the background for much of Scheler's other writings.[2] We discuss this question here in order to show its relevance to Scheler's whole theory of sociology and to appreciate the applications which Scheler made in his theory on the sociology of knowledge.

FORMS OF SOCIALITY

At the very core of Scheler's sociology lay his theory of person as originally developed in *Formalism*. He strongly maintained that the being (*Sein*) of the person was the very intrinsic end (*Ziel*) of all community and of all historical evolution. Therefore, while he was forced to modify Kant's "Person of Reason" and Nietzsche's theory of "Great Men," he accepted their emphasis upon *persons* as ultimate bearers of the highest values. Scheler opposed all types of positivism,

---

[1] *Ibid.*, 23-51.
[2] Cf. *Wissensformen*, 33–44, where the four forms of human society are briefly described.

historicism, capitalism and Marxism which sacrificed the higher ethical values of the person for some other supposed end (*Zweck*) of pure progress or of an ideal state.[1] This was a common critique for Scheler; we have already seen one place in *Forms of Knowledge* where it appeared.[2]

In describing in finer detail the ethical dimensions of the person, Scheler made capital point of the individuality of the person. The individual person, as a pure individualistic spirit, is the ultimate bearer of ethical values. In his most intimate being, the person is a moral being. Essentially, therefore, a person must be an ethical being before he can possess legal, political and economic rights. This proposition must not be isolated from the rest of Scheler's social theory, for as it stands, the statement may sound like a thesis from modern theories of political and economic liberalism. There is a definite distinction between Scheler's theory of the individuality of persons and modern theories of individualism.

In the last chapter we discussed in some detail Scheler's theory of the individuation of persons.[3] The important point here is to note the close interplay between man's individuality and his social nature. Scheler contended that man's primary experience went out towards others, towards social groups, and only subsequently could man isolate his own Self from the *we* of the community. The strict individuation of persons as concrete centers of spiritual activity in no way contradicted the social nature of man. The state or an economic society could never arise by contract if man were not a social being originally and essentially. It was in this sense that Scheler opposed Hobbes and Rousseau and theories of modern liberalism.[4]

The collective unity of the communal *we* in all its collective togetherness was defined by Scheler as being a collective social person (*Gesamtperson*). Just as the being of an individualized person (*das Sein der Person*) and his world is constituted in its own individual acts, so is the being of the collective person (*das Sein der Gesamtperson*) and its world constituted in its own special essential class of social acts. Such a joint person (*Verbandsperson*) and its world is an experienced reality of people living together within a unified social group. The collective person is not just a mental construct, it is not just a world created by the compilation of individual worlds. The collective person is a unified experience of the

---

[1] *Formalismus*, 507–10.
[2] Cf. *supra*, n. 7.
[3] Cf. Ch. III, sect. 2.
[4] *Formalismus*, 512–23.

whole social group living together as a single unit, as a family, a tribe or a nation.[1]

The most basic bond of unity within the collective person is the *moral solidarity* which the whole group experiences. Through moral solidarity each person feels a moral responsibility for its own particular collective group as such, as well as a co-responsibility for all the individual persons within that group. Therefore, not only is the collective person individualized in the very acts by which it is essentially constituted a *Gesamtperson* in the first place, but also, through the principle of moral solidarity, the collective person itself becomes a bearer of genuine moral values. In other words, just as the single person (*Einzelperson*) is totally individualized in itself and is the ultimate bearer of value, so the collective person (*Gesamtperson*) is also individualized through its own constituting act and is itself a bearer of genuine ethical values.

The spirit and method of Scheler's phenomenology controlled his whole approach to the question concerning the sociality of man. Therefore, this was not a mere study of the contingent, historical order of things, but a study of the universal, *a priori* objective order of social facts. Scheler's own version of Robinson Crusoe returned repeatedly as an example of a man who was essentially a being-in-community, but who had not experienced a particular, concrete member of his community. In this spirit, Scheler defined four basic *forms* of man's sociality. These were described in universal terms as four essentially different types of social groups or collective persons according to which men gather together into groups. These are four different *forms* which the interaction between the individual person (*Einzelperson*) and the collective person (*Gesamtperson*) can take.

The first and lowest social unity is that of the *herd* among animals and that of the *mass* among men. As Scheler explained in *Sympathy*, the mass is constituted through emotional infection with an involuntary following of a particular emotional movement.[2] The mass is a social group lower than community. Yet it has an individual constitution of its own and its own particular reality. While the bond of strict moral solidarity does not exist in the mass, it does possess its own degree of legal and moral responsibility. Some naturalistic theories of man's social nature are so dependent upon evolutionary biological principles that they consider man's life in community to be nothing more than a difference in degree from the emotional, impulsive society in the mass.

[1] *Ibid.*, 524–27.
[2] Cf. Ch. III, sect. 1.

Scheler's anthropology demanded a higher and an essentially different type of community for man, due to the fact that the presence of spirit in man makes man an essentially different being from brutes. Therefore, in *Formalism*, the discussion on the social form of the mass is very short.[1]

The second type of social unity outlined by Scheler is that of life-community (*Lebensgemeinschaft*). This he called the "pure" community: it is the first consciously experienced social group around us. We immediately find ourselves living with one another. All our common acts of seeing, hearing, loving, hating are naturally unified in their constitution of this basic life-community. The common examples of life-community are the family, the tribe, and the nation. The life-community cherishes its own values and strives immediately for its own intrinsic ends (*Ziele*). This is the primary instance of a collective person (*Gesamtperson*) joined by the bond of moral solidarity. The life-community is completely automatic and unreflective in its choice of values and ends. The values and ends of life-community, which are authentic personal values, are realized throughout the entire social group as a single unity. Life-community is essentially antecedent to all social or economic contracts and to all deliberately planned societies.[2]

In contrast to life-community, Scheler carefully defined his meaning of *society* (*Gesellschaft*). The social unity of society is deliberately planned, an association; in this sense, it is an *artificial* unity. The end (*Zweck*) of society is consciously known and sought after by the individual persons who join together by contract to achieve the particular goal of that society. Society seeks sub-personal values; for example, society as a social unity seeks *pleasant* values for its members, society as the bearer of civilization seeks *useful* values.

As we have seen, in the essential order of essences, society is based upon community. While there can be no society without an antecedent community, community is possible without the deliberate association of society. Only through moral solidarity in community do promises and contracts become meaningful in the first place. Therefore, every contractual society depends upon community. Society functions through its own devised rules. It is ruled by the numerical vote of the majority of the individuals within the society.[3]

---

[1] *Formalismus*, 529.

[2] *Ibid.*, 529–31.

[3] *Ibid.*, 531–36. The fundamental difference between *Gemeinschaft* and *Gesellschaft* was the chief contribution to sociology by Ferdinand Tönnies in his book entitled *Gemeinschaft und Gesellschaft*, originally published in 1887 (eighth edition appeared in 1935); cf. Tönnies,

The fourth form of social groups is that of the *person-community* (*Person-gemeinschaft*), the religious group, which is united by a solidarity of salvation. This principle is the basic article of the world of finite moral persons in the realm of finite persons. Within the religious community, responsibility is not so much for the individual members of the community, but there exists a co-responsibility for the total group as a unit, in the sense of a common salvation, a common good, a common evil, a common guilt. Just as some common social *life*, in the wide sense of the term, is the basis for life-community, so a spiritual *love* at the strictly personal level is the foundation for person-community. This love and the whole salvational community find their total fulfillment only in God, the Person of Persons.[1] We will discuss this most perfect type of community after our study on Scheler's theory of love.[2]

The terms *community, collective person* and *solidarity* seem slightly ambiguous for Scheler. On the one hand, his general definitions of community and collective person included the essential notion of some moral solidarity. But on the other hand, only person-community, the most perfect type of community, fulfills the original definition of community and moral person. We have already noted that the mass in itself does not fulfill the strict requirements of either community or collective person. Furthermore, life-community is only an inchoative community; it is not strictly a collective *person*, it does not possess a strict moral solidarity at the personal-salvational level. Life-community corresponds to the body-*I*, as the person-community corresponds to the person. Only at the strictly spiritual level does the true transcendence of the person stand out. Only at this point is the collective group a collective *person* (*Gesamtperson*) and is the bond of solidarity between them a strictly moral solidarity of love and salvation. As a matter of fact, human society is never a mere life-community and never a purely formalistic society, but always a group of *persons* living together. The ultimate bond of unity between men (and, essentially, the most basic foundation for all sociality) is the bond of salvational solidarity in person-community.

Community and Association, translated and supplemented by Charles P. Loomis (London: Routledge & Kegan Paul Ltd., 1955); see especially the Foreword by Pitrim Sorokin and the Translator's Introduction, v–xxvii. It is to be noted that Loomis translates *Gesellschaft* as *association*, instead of *society*, but he, too, is apologetical about the terms (xviii), and throughout the work retains the German terms *Gemeinschaft* and *Gesellschaft* within the text itself.

[1] *Formalismus*, 536–42. Scheler's description of *Persongemeinschaft* as distinct from, and essentially superior, to *Lebensgemeinschaft* is a further elaboration upon the *Gemeinschaft*-theory of Tönnies.

[2] Cf. Vh. V, sect. 4.

These four forms of sociality re-appeared frequently in Scheler's thought, and, especially, of course, in his sociological writings. One prime instance of this was his theory concerning the sociology of knowledge.

THE SOCIOLOGY OF KNOWLEDGE

The terms themselves about the sociology of knowledge as well as the original theory were a special contribution to contemporary thought by Max Scheler.[1] Scheler's understanding of the science of sociology and his classification of man into various social groups led him to the further investigation of the sociology of knowledge. Man's activity of knowing is obviously an outcome of spirit in man. Moreover, knowing is not just an individual activity; the community in which man lives influences the very mode and content of his knowledge. Therefore, just as there are universal classes of essential social groups, so also each individual group will have its own distinct essential type of knowledge. Once Scheler had defined sociology in terms of a phenomenological investigation, then the sociology of knowledge was necessarily a part of cultural sociology.

Scheler devided the problems of a sociology of knowledge into two classes: formal problems and material problems. Among the formal problems there were the questions about the relationship of the sociology of knowledge to logic and epistemology, the relationship of man's knowledge to his social nature and the original classification of social knowledge into its predominant kinds. The material problems of a sociology of knowledge dealt directly with the major types of knowledge (religious, metaphysical and scientific) and a number of more detailed problems within these classes.

Our own study cannot give a detailed exposition of Scheler's sociology of knowledge. We will merely sketch the outlines of Scheler's theory in order to see here the consistency in the application of many of his dominant ideas. This is one area of Scheler's thought in which he deliberately sought a general synthesis between the many diverse

---

[1] Cf. J. Macquet, *The Sociology of Knowledge: Its Structure and Its Relation to the Philosophy of Knowledge: A Critical Analysis of the Systems of Karl Mannheim and Petrim A. Sorokin*, translated by John F. Locke, with a Preface by F. S. C. Northrop (Boston: The Beacon Press, 1951), Chapter One, "Introduction," 9, 19–28; K. Mannheim, *Essays on the Sociology of Knowledge*, edited by Paul Kecskemeti (London: Routledge & Kegan Paul Ltd., 1952), 1–27. It is to be noted that Mannheim's first essay on this topic, *Sociology of Knowledge*, appeared in 1925 and is primarily a discussion of Scheler's earlier work "Problem's for a Sociology of Knowledge" of 1924. This Essay of Mannheim's is reprinted in the present volume, Ch. IV, "The Problem of a Sociology of Knowledge," 134–190. Part three, 154–179 discusses Scheler's theory.

directions his studies of man, metaphysics, history and science had taken. At times, it seems, Scheler forced his own categories upon the available evidence. Yet many of his isolated ideas become clearer and more meaningful when they are compared by way of agreement or disagreement with the rest of his thought. We cannot fail but to be impressed with the breadth of the comprehension of Scheler's thought.

Scheler's sociology of knowledge rested upon three chief axioms. These axioms were not proved here but merely taken over from other studies. The first axion was the phenomenologically established truth that man is genetically and consciously a member of community *before* he is conscious of his own Self as an *I*. I know myself to be a member of a *we* before I know my Self as an individual *I*.[1] This was the fundamental truth discussed in Part Three of *Sympathy*. This was the most basic truth of man's social nature.

The second axiom held that participation in the experiences of others occurred in different ways with different groups, but that these different "ways" could be classified according to certain ideal types. Reference here was to the four various forms of social structure: the mass, life-community, society and person-community. Man shows his essential superiority to lower animals by his ability to understand (*verstehen*) the meaning of his social experience and to translate and communicate his understanding through language.[2]

At this point, Scheler distinguished between the *spirit* (*Geist*) and the *soul* (*Seele*) of a group as two sociologically significant principles. The *group soul* is, as it were, an organic development. Spontaneously but unconsciously, it expresses itself by working from within the group to such external expressions as myths, fairy tales, folk songs and group mores. The group soul is anonymous and impersonal in its creation. The *group spirit* also works spontaneously, but it is conscious of its intentional objects. Personal representatives are responsible for the group spirit; while only a small number, the elite, they become the exemplars, the leaders of the group spirit and work from above to influence the group. The results of the group spirit are art, science, philosophy, the state, a cultural language.[3]

The third basic principle for the sociology of knowledge involved a

---

[1] *Wissensformen*, 52. Cf. Part Three of *Sympathy* and much of our discussion above in Ch. III.

[2] *Wissensformen*, 53.

[3] *Ibid.*, 53–55. "Group soul" is closely associated with both "life and person-community," carrying with it the dynamism of the vital impulse into "we" community. "Group spirit" also has the note of spontaneity and authenticity about it; it is not the mere artificial creation of *society*.

basic epistemological theory concerning the relationship and the ordering of our knowledge with reality. To clarify this point, Scheler undertook a short schematic review of the various spheres of intentionality and their order of intentional dependence. The spheres of being and objects (*Seins – und Gegenstandsphäre*) are fivefold: 1. The absolute sphere of reality, values and of the holy; 2. the sphere of a co-world (*Mitwelt*), a world shared with others, the sphere of society and history; 3. the spheres of the outer and inner world, i.e., of one's own body and of his environmental world; 4. the sphere of the living; 5. the sphere of the inorganic and of the seemingly dead world. These spheres are irreducible to one another; all are equally and originally given in human consciousness. There is, however, an essential order in the givenness of these spheres. This order Scheler described through his five "laws of pregivenness"; by this, he meant to describe the order in which these various essential spheres are consciously entertained in intentionality. 1. The outer world is pre-given to the inner world. 2. The living world is pre-given to the dead world. 3. The outer world of the co-subjects of my social world is pre-given to the inner world of my own social world. 4. The inner world of the social world is pre-given to my own inner world. 5. My own body and every alien body is pre-given as a *field of expression* (not a body-object [*Körpergegenstand*]) to all subsequent distinctions between body and soul.

These laws are nothing more than a continuation of many of the principles discussed in Part Three of *Sympathy*. Immediately relevant to the sociology of knowledge is the fundamental proposition that the social sphere, the world of togetherness shared with others (*Mitwelt*), is historically the world pre-given to all the other spheres. The social world, therefore, is antecedent to the basic reality of life itself or to any other general or definite intentional content.[1]

The first and most general application of these laws for the sociology of knowledge was to emphasize the social character of all knowledge. Not only the content of knowledge and the very choice of objects are conditioned by the dominating social interests, but the *forms* of the spiritual acts of knowledge themselves are necessarily sociological and are mutually conditioned in and through the structure of the society in which they occur.[2]

With these principles Scheler could discuss how the chief kinds of

---

[1] *Ibid.*, 55–57.

[2] *Ibid.*, 58. For a very accurate exposition of this matter cf. P. A. Schilpp, "The 'Formal Problem' of Scheler's Sociology of Knowledge," *The Philosophical Review*, 36 (March, 1927), 101–20.

knowledge are related to their social context and social background. Space allows here only a general description of Scheler's detailed discussions on "the sociology of religion," "the sociology of metaphysics" and "the sociology of the positive sciences." Basic to these more specialized kinds of knowledge was the more general knowledge of the common man, the natural attitude of the natural *Weltanschauung*. Scheler adopted a position he described as a theory of a "relative natural *Weltanschauung*." Whatever is accepted as validly given without question in a particular group is part of that group's *Weltanschauung*. This, then, becomes part of the *group soul*. Scheler held that there was no absolute, unchanging natural *Weltanschauung* of man in some state of pure nature. Every civilization creates its own world outlook.[1]

Distinct from the more general natural attitude of the common man are the specialized knowledges of religion, metaphysics and scientific technology. Each type of knowledge has its social origin and social development in historical time and place. But the three types of knowledge are the result of the essential, permanent essence of the human spirit; they are *not* three stages of a single historical-temporal sequential evolution of human development as Comte thought.[2] The three types of knowledge are distinguished by the different motives from which they spring, by different knowing acts, by different intrinsic ends, by different types of models and exemplars and by the different social groups in which the form of knowledge occurs.[3]

The sociology of knowledge studies in detail the last point; namely, a study of the three different social forms of knowledge as related to distinct social groups. Scheler listed six points in this study. 1. The different ideal types of leaders or models in each type of knowledge: the *homo religiosus*, the wise man, the scientific researcher. 2. The different original sources and methods of each type of knowledge: through immediate contact with the divine, through essential-ideal modes of philosophic thought, through the inductive and deductive conclusions of science. 3. The different forms of development: this is a sociological study of the essential forms of intrinsic development within a science, and not a mere historical study of concrete facts. 4. The different basic

---

[1] Scheler accepted the natural attitude of the common man without depreciating it, as Husserl had done. Scheler also accepted from Dilthey a "relative natural *Weltanschauung*," without subjecting it to Husserl's rigorous investigation. Cr. Husserl's *Logos* essay of 1910, "Philosophy as a Strict Science," translated by Q. Lauer, S.J., *Cross Currents*, 6, 227–46, 325–44.

[2] Cf. *Soziologie*, 30–31.

[3] *Ibid.*, 33–34. Cf. also "Vorbilder und Führer," *Nachlass*, 255–343.

social forms in which the knowledges present themselves: e.g., as incorporated in the traditions of the people, inscribed in ceremonies or rites, or written down in books and taught by the schools. 5. The different functions of the varous types of knowledge in human society. 6. The different sociological classes from which the various kinds of knowledge have sprung.[1]

Most of Scheler's major works on religion, sociology, epistemology and education were written within this schema as devised by the sociology of knowledge. But while the schema purported to be all-encompassing, it failed to be completely satisfactory. Not only was it inadequate to explain all the relevant data, but Scheler continued to modify some of the basic divisions in the schema. Thus, by 1928 he stated that the three basic kinds of knowledge were: the knowledge of control and achievement (technology), the knowledge of essence or culture (philosophy) and the knowledge of metaphysical reality or salvation.[2] This denoted a change not only in the general outline for a sociology of knowledge, but a more radical change in the meaning of philosophy, metaphysics and religion.[3]

This treatment has high-lighted only the most general principles of Scheler's sociology. The essentially social nature of man gave Scheler a theory on the sociology of knowledge and a classification of four different *forms* of man's sociality—the mass, life-community, society and person-community. However, the study of man's togetherness can be studied scientifically and phenomenologically in another way. We can study in an essential way the individual *ways* or *modes* by which men live together. As a matter of fact, Scheler first made his phenomenological studies on such social "feelings" as sympathy, shame, love and hatred, and only later expanded his views on sociology itself. We have reversed the chronology of Scheler's studies to show the inner consistency of his thought and to explain better the meaning and significance of Scheler's phenomenology of community.

---

[1] *Wissensformen*, 68.
[2] *Perspectives*, 1–12; *Weltanschauung*, 5–15.
[3] Cf. *supra*, Ch. I, sect. 3.

CHAPTER FIVE

MAN AND COMMUNITY

Scheler's early phenomenology was especially directed to the investigation of the essential *a priori* structures of emotional experiences. Among these were the social emotions which he later weaved into his whole theory of sociology. According to Scheler's epistemology, *perception* also includes affective and emotional "feelings," so that the perception of others includes the affective "feelings" we experience in our living together with others. The more important "social feelings" are those of sympathy, shame and love. Love, however, occurs only at the strictly transcendental level of persons who live together in person-community. Scheler's entire theory of man, sociology and religion reaches its climax in his description of person-community living together with love and within salvational solidarity.

SYMPATHY

Although Scheler used the Greek-stemmed term, *Sympathie*, in the title of his study, his most common term is the strictly German equivalent, *Mitgefühl*.[1] The 1913 title, "The Phenomenology and Theory of the Feeling of Sympathy," more explicitly stated the method of procedure; namely, that this was a phenomenological investigation into the *feeling* of sympathy. The 1923 title emphasized the outline-result of the study: a description of the "essence and forms of sympathy." The aim of our exposition of Scheler's theory of sympathy is to distinguish clearly this emotion from all its mistaken alternates, to describe the inner laws and interactions of sympathetic functions and to explain its relation to moral value. From such a study we will see how Scheler understood sympathy to be a basic emotion of man's social life.

Mitgefühl is literally a "feeling with" some one else. In the English translation by Heath, this term is consistently translated as "fellow-

---

[1] *Sympathy* in Greek is composed of *sym*, "with," and *pathos*, "suffering, passion"; therefore, it means literally a "feeling with" someone. *Compassion* in its Latin stems has the same basic meaning. The German is *Mit-gefühl*. There is no immediate English equivalent.

feeling." Fellow-feeling involves two poles of intentional reference. There is first of all a reference to the actual emotional state of the individualized other Self. But this other-reference can take place only within the background of the consciousness of my own Self as individualized. *I* sympathize with another in the perception of *his own* emotional state and in my co-responding with *him* and his emotions and not to mine. Both his Self and mine are recognized to be individualized centers of self-consciousness.[1]

For example, A is in grief over the death of his mother. B commiserates with A—literally, is "sorry with" A. Phenomenologically speaking, these are two distinct facts. A's grief is not B's; B need not (indeed, *can*not) experience A's own individual emotion. But B does genuinely sympathize with A when B feels in A the grief that A himself feels. In the response of authentic sympathy, B in some real way actually participates in, "takes a part with," the grief of A.

It is false to say that B cannot sympathize with A unless he actually knows "what it is to lose your mother." It would be unrealistic and selfish of A to demand that B must first lose his own mother *before* he can feel the sorrow of A's loss. It is true that somehow, somewhere in B's past, he has identified himself with the feeling of grief-over-mother's death, so that he can reproduce this feeling in his sympathy with A. But in B's fellow-feeling with A, B feels this grief as suffered by A. In another case, C may arrive and say: "Ah, yes, I remember when *my* mother died!" C may shed copious tears—but he is emotionally reliving his own loss and in no way is he *suffering with* A in A's grief.[2]

Scheler carefully distinguished true fellow-feeling from "community of feeling" (*Mit-einanderfühlen*). If a father and mother have lost a child in death, they both feel the same sorrow and the same painful loss. They share a feeling in common, but in this loss they do not actually sympathize with each other. A third party may arrive to express com-

---

[1] *Sympathie*, 9–11; *Sympathy*, 13–14. It is interesting to note that Scheler's description of sympathy (and of *love* at the personal level) as involving two distinct poles of intentional reference accepts a formula very similar to a key principle of Thomistic epistemology. St. Thomas speaks of knowledge as the union with the other as other. Scheler speaks of sympathizing with and loving the other *as other*. Both use this experience as primary in their refutation of monism and in the acceptance of reality.

[2] English words by which we "want to express our sympathy" limp badly in conveying the depths of feeling we actually feel in such a situation. If "condolences" retained its Latin stem meaning it would be the equivalent of the German *Mitleid*, a "sorrowing with." We say: "With deepest sympathy!" A common German phrase is: *mit innigster (tiefster) Teilnahme*. A literal rendering of these phrases would be: "Deep within myself I take part in (I feel) the sorrow you feel!" As Heidegger has reworked the etymology of language to re-discover the language of metaphysics, a similar study could be made to bring life and meaning back to our common terms about the emotions and especially about the social emotions.

passion with both parents in true sympathy. A community feeling, one in essence but shared in together equality by several persons, is possible only at the mental (*seelisch*) level. Bodily pain and physically pleasant feelings are exclusively individual. No two men suffer the same identical physical pain or feeling of sense pleasure. The second man can only suffer *with* the first man's physical pain or rejoice *over* the first man's good bodily feelings.[1]

   Sympathy, both as a meaningful term and as an actual emotional experience, must not be taken to mean only a "feeling with another *in pain.*" Sympathy is a generic thing. It includes not only the two sub-species of a "sorrowing with" and a "rejoicing with" but also any number of actual emotional responses between two people.[2] When F inflicts an act of cruelty upon G, F takes pleasure in the pain of G. Here is a genuine case of fellow-feeling in which F is wholly aware of and responsive to the emotional state of G. In cases of brutality, in spite of the fact that F is sensitive to the suffering of G, F continues the particular brutal activity. One cannot be cruel or brutal to a stone or to any "dead" object. He must perceive a vital emotional response on the part of the object.[3] Scheler held that a man can be cruel and brutal (in a strictly immoral way) to plants and animals, for in them is life.

   In this context, Scheler was able to distinguish genuine fellow-feeling from emotional infection (*Gefühlsansteckung*) and from emotional identification (*Einfühlung*). These two explanations were proposed by various scientific, genetic theories to account for man' social nature. We have already seen Scheler's general criticism against them.[4] Both theories failed to give proper credit to the two-fold polarity between the *I* and the Thou which is an essential element of the phenomenological understanding of the emotion of true sympathy. Emotional infection (e.g., of a mob) does not allow me to know the other and sympathize with him

---

[1] *Sympathie*, 9; *Sympathy*, 12–13.
[2] Cf. Ch. IX of Part One, "Pity and Rejoicing and its Typical Modes," *Sympathie*, 149–51; *Sympathy*, 135–37. Here, again, Scheler undertook a piece of etymology to get his meaning across. *Mitgefühle* includes both *Mitleid* (pity, "suffer with") and *Mitfreude* ("rejoicing with"). German regularly employs only the former term; Scheler was forced to coin the word meaning "rejoicing with." One of Schopenhauer's mistakes was to take pity (*Mitleid*) as the generic emotion instead of seeing that both follow-pity and fellow-rejoicing are sub-species of fellow-feeling.
[3] *Sympathie*, 10–11; *Sympathy*, 14.
[4] Cf. *supra*, Ch. III. H. Becker, "Some Forms of Sympathy: A Phenomenological Analysis," *The Journal of Abnormal and Social Psychology*, 6 (1931–32), 58–68, is a brief but good exposition of the core of Scheler's positive theory of sympathy. Becker's original attempt to translate Scheler's ideas into English is quite satisfactory, but the terms that Heath employed in the published translation of *Sympathy* are beginning to be adopted as standard. V. J. McGill's essay, "Scheler's Theory of Sympathy and Love," *Philosophy and Phenomenological Research*, 2 (1942), 173–91, is a poor study of Scheler's theory of sympathy.

in his situation: I am simply swept into the other's situation. In emotional identification (e.g., with a hypnotist), I again lose my own self individuality. True sympathy must retain both the individuality of myself and the other, as I "take part in" *his* emotional state of soul.

Scheler asked if there was an essential order of dependence between the various social emotions connected with sympathy.[1] This is a question of strict phenomenology in which there is analyzed the relationship, the essential laws (*ein wesengesetzliches Verhältnis*), of the connections between the various emotions. Scheler attempted to define the *a priori* order and dependence of the various emotional functions. His own discussion is very sketchy and unsatisfactory. We will attempt to fill in the details of his outline.

A common social response is to repeat and reproduce in oneself the emotion he perceives in another. Scheler described such an emotional response as *Nachfühlen* or *Nachleben*, a "feeling or living *after*" one has experienced a particular emotion in another. This is a case of vicarious feeling.[2] It is to be distinguished from both empathy and genuine sympathy. In reproduced feeling we sense the *quality* of another's feeling, e.g., his sorrow, without participating in his sorrow (as in the case of true fellow-feeling) or without being infected with it. We may say: "I know how you feel, but I cannot sympathize with you." A novelist possesses to a high degree the ability to visualize and reproduce the feelings of others, without sharing those emotions with others.[3]

The first law of dependence between emotional functions is that reproduced feeling can only follow upon some antecedent identification with that feeling. At some previous time, I must have felt the *quality* of sorrow before I can reproduce this feeling, either by memory of myself or through some response to the sorrow of others. Thus, children and primitives first live at the level of emotional identification before they advance to the stage of vicarious feeling. A young child at play with her doll *feels* herself *to be* a mother; an older child will only reproduce vicariously the role of mother. Primitives first are *one* with their ancestors before they develop a cult of them. Aesthetic empathy of the theater (which is a feeling whereby one puts himself *along side of another*) is a further development of reproduced feeling, a distance removed from the total emotional identification employed in early mystic rites or by children.

---

[1] *Sympathie*, 105; *Sympathy*, 96. This, then, is the study of the next two chapters of the work.

[2] Heath translates these two terms in various ways: "vicarious feeling," "reproduction of feeling or experience," "reproduced emotion."

[3] *Sympathie*, 3–5; *Sympathy*, 8–10.

Obviously, for Scheler, there is no such thing as innate knowledge of emotional states. All of our knowledge of feelings is gathered only from the actual experience of those feelings. We must become one with a feeling, be identified with it, consciously or unconsciously, before we can ever recognize or reproduce this feeling either in ourselves or in others. Quite literally, a child *is* a mother through emotional identification before it can feel like one. The mystery religions and the myths of the primitives are rich in meaning for the ontogenetic understanding of man as well as for the study of phylogenesis. By 1922 Scheler was somewhat acquainted with Jung's works. In theory and spirit, Scheler was prepared to entertain the chief hypothesis of Jung.[1]

A second law is that vicarious feeling is an antecedent foundation for true fellow-feeling.[2] I cannot "feel with" another unless I reproduce the emotion I perceive in him. It is to be noted that this is not a conscious series of steps. In an act of true sympathy I respond spontaneously to the peculiar emotional state of the other person. However, in the final phenomenological analysis that act of sympathy rests upon some prior act of reproduced emotion.

The third law of dependence is that fellow-feeling is a necessary condition for the possible emergence of benevolence.[3] To explain this law, Scheler revealed some more keen insights into the essence of fellow-feeling itself. We can sympathize only with a *real* subject. It is the act of fellow-feeling that perceives the reality of the subject. Therefore, while we can reproduce a vicarious emotion for a fictional hero, we can have no true sympathy for that hero. Also, in the pure act of fellow-feeling, we do not advert to any special values of the other subject. Indeed, we can sympathize with non-human subjects.

Scheler's meaning for *benevolence* shifted with the context. In polemical passages (e.g., in most of *Ressentiment*), benevolence was equated with humanitarianism and philanthropy. By this Scheler meant a condescending attitude of a man towards the whole of mankind as a species and which looked out especially for the material welfare of mankind. As a more common and better definition for benevo-

---

[1] *Sympathie*, 105–07; *Sympathy*, 96–98. In *Sympathy*, Scheler accepted Jung's extension of Freud's theory of *libido* to include any striving whatsoever. Scheler did not, however, elaborate upon Jung's use of popular myths as sources of information for the understanding of the full meaning of man. But here in the study of emotional identification, Scheler's thought is similar to Jung's and may have been influenced by the reading of *Die Wandlungsform der Libido* to which Scheler has reference in footnotes. See C. J. Jung, *Psychology of the Unconscious* (New York: Moffat, Yard and Company, 1917).

[2] *Sympathie*, 107; *Sympathy*, 98.

[3] *Sympathie*, 107–08; *Sympathy*, 98–99.

lence, Scheler understood it to mean a genuine movement of love towards all of mankind in view of a common humanity. The former (exaggerated) idea of benevolence arose from *ressentiment*: the latter Scheler conceded to be a genuine human sentiment, but essentially inferior to Christian love.[1]

The meaning of Scheler's third law is this. The unity of mankind as a species must be first realized emotionally through fellow-feeling in all its concreteness as a felt intentional act before true benevolence is possible.

The fourth law of dependence is that benevolence is the basis for all personal love and for the love of God. This means that one must feel a generalized love for the total species of mankind (and not just one's friends, one's countrymen, etc.) before he can have the individualized spiritual love of persons. The Christian love of persons, historically, was built upon the *humanitas* of the ancient classical ethos. Scheler called this a "non-cosmic" love of persons and of God, to distinguish it from the strictly vitalistic theories of love and from the many forms of Oriental cosmic mysticism.

This fourth law transcends the order of merely sympathetic feelings, for it entails necessarily the spirituality of person and the fact of persons living in community. This, in turn, entails further laws of dependence. Real personal love depends upon benevolence, but at the same time, love is possible only through a prior condition of love *for* God and a love *in* God. The full meaning of this statement will become clear only after we understand Scheler's theory of love and his theory of a spiritual-personal community.

Scheler felt that all this discussion about emotion, their metaphysical significance and their laws of dependence gave him ample foundation to "moralize" about the *ideal* normative order of values. This would be a distinct contribution to ethics, to education and to civilization in general. Thus, one ideal norm he proposed is that man must cultivate *all* his various emotional powers, if he is to achieve the full realization of his ideal capacities.[3]

Scheler's prime concern was that man must reunite himself in an intrinsic living way with the lower powers of life and of nature itself. The vital values are the lowest in the scale of values, but they are the most powerful, the most real. Man would undermine his own being if

---

[1] One of the sections of this present chapter will treat of Scheler's theory of love. His essay *Ressentiment* is an extended study on the false values of humanitarianism.

[2] *Sympathie*, 108–12; *Sympathy*, 99–102.

[3] *Sympathie*, 112–13; *Sympathy*, 103–04.

he cultivated only the spiritual and intellectual powers at the expense of his lower, vitalistic, emotional nature.[1] Scheler's criticism here was directed against the rationalists and the natural scientists: both groups artificially cut themselves off from nature, to study nature and to control it.[2] Historically, the first "scientist" was always the enthusiastic amateur who began his study of nature in an emotional state whereby he identified himself with nature. The mystic astrologist preceded the astronomer. The "expert" only arrives late and he debases his humanity if he lose living contact with the "enthusiast."[3]

As we have seen, Scheler did not assent to the Oriental ethos to the extent of advocating total emotional identity with the living universe. He sought a reciprocal adjustment between the ethos of the East with that of the West. The Oriental ethos should be counter-balanced with the western ideals of benevolence and *humanitas*. We of the West should learn from the East how to cultivate in ourselves a love for Mother Nature.[4]

In pleading for man's return to cosmic unity with nature, Scheler criticized the effects of industrialization and technology (a consequence of science's knowledge of domination) which seek only production of material goods at the sacrifice of not only organic values (destruction of natural resources) but also at the sacrifice of human, personal values.[5]

[1] *Sympathie*, 113–16; *Sympathy*, 104–06.

[2] This discussion integrates much of Scheler's thought on man, nature, the different types of knowledge and philosophy. He states here in anticipation of *Man's Place*: "It is man the microcosm, an actual embodiment of the reality of existence in *all* its forms, who is himself *cosmomorphic*, and as such the possessor of sources of *insight* into all that is comprised in the nature of the cosmos." *Sympathy*, 105. If man so intellectualizes nature to lose his emotional identification with it, he cuts himself off from the living sources of his own vitality. This idea returns in Scheler's fluctuating definitions of philosophy and in his final definition of metaphysics that includes this vital "salvational" unity with the life-impulse in nature. Further application in the areas of education and culture are made in his 1925 address, "The Forms of Knowledge and Culture," *Perspectives*, 13–49; *Weltanschauung*, 16–48.

[3] A continuation of this theme in Scheler's studies on models and leaders in human history—the hero, the genius, the saint. These are not studied as abstract models. Their real import is carried by the fact that historically they have realized in themselves—they have made *real* within the content of the living concrete details of actual history—the military, intellectual and religious *ideals* of man. See "Vorbilder und Führer" *in Nachlass*, 255–343.

[4] This general idea of adjustment was taken as a topic of another address, "Man in the Era of Adjustment," delivered in 1927. See *Perspectives*, 94–125; *Weltanschauung*, 89–118. It is here that Scheler speaks of human higher cult as a "re-sublimation" in order to renew its contacts with the living and the real.

[5] In Scheler's plea for man and civilization to return to an emotional identification with all of cosmic life ("for there is ultimately *one* life only, and *one* vital value which comprehends all living things," *Sympathy*, 106) he comes very close to the pure, simple principle of Albert Schweitzer, who in his "Reverence for Life" principle proposed to build a genuinely ethical civilization. Cf. A. Schweitzer, *The Philosophy of Civilization* (New York: MacMillan, 1960), esp., Chapters 26 and 27, 307–44. Neither Scheler nor Schweitzer make any explicit reference to each other, but there is a kindred spirit between them. H. Marcuse, in *Eros and Civilization* (New York: Vintage Books, 1962), advocates a similar return of man's natural and spon-

Life and its immediate values can be sacrified for higher spiritual and religious values, but Scheler considered a "martyr to science" as being ridiculous. Wealth and material goods are to be put to the service of the physical and mental health of the whole human family.

The third and fourth laws of the dependence of emotional functions were invoked to describe *how* man was to effect his immersion into the total stream of life. Man can first enter into such an identification with life only at that point where life is in closest affinity to his own, namely, in *another person* and, ultimately, only in God. Only if man has experienced the emotional union between man and man will he be able to find the living, dynamic side of Nature.[1] The full phenomenological understanding of infancy, childhood and youth would reveal the true meanings involved in the totality of human experience. Scheler himself undertook a detailed phenomenological study of the sexual act in all its intrinsic, vital and personal ends (*Ziele*), to restore the idea of the sexual act to its true metaphysical significance as a personal act of man in contact and in union with cosmic life.[2] In this context, Scheler discussed the sexual act as a part of man's sympathetic function with the living cosmos, and not as a special part of personal love.

A final consideration is the study of the *moral value* of fellow-feeling. Scheler declared that all genuine acts of sympathy have positive moral values in their own right. He approved the common adage: "A sorrow shared is a sorrow halved; a joy shared is a joy doubled." A mark of genuine sympathy is that it leads to acts of true benevolence.

The degree of moral value of an act of sympathy is relative to the four following conditions. 1) The moral value is relative to the level of the sympathetic emotion; e.g., sympathy with a sensory, vital, mental (*seelisch*) or spiritual emotion. 2) Sympathy, in the sense of community of feeling with someone, or through emotional infection, only increases quantitatively the particular emotion present. This, as such, has no positive moral value. 3) The moral value of fellow-feeling increases to the extent that it is directed to the very center of the person's personality and not towards some merely external circumstances. 4) The

taneous allignment with the primitive drives of his nature through a type of civilization he calls (in Freudian terms) a non-repressive civilization, in which sublimation is attained, not in the repression of the lower drives, but by having Eros attain its objectives, transcend its immediate lower level and search for its fuller gratification at higher levels.

[1] *Sympathie*, 117–18; *Sympathy*, 107–08.

[2] *Sympathie*, 120–43; *Sympathy*, 109–29. Another study on this topic, with all the insights of phenomenology but with a Catholic theological point of view, is the work by Scheler's student, Dietrich Von Hildebrand, *In Defense of Purity: An Analysis of the Catholic Ideals of Purity and Virginity* (New York: Longman's, Green and Co., 1931).

moral value varies according to the worth of the whole situation; e.g., it is better to sympathize with a person of superior values. Scheler accredited important moral value to fellow-feeling, but consistently denied that it alone was the *source* of moral value.[1]

SHAME

The sense of shame is one of man's social characteristics. A study of Scheler's theory of shame and the feeling of shame makes a fine transition between a study of man in his body-self dimension (where occur the sympathetic *functions*) and the study of man as person (at which level occur the genuine *acts* of love). The different forms of shame encompass both these levels in man. The sense of shame is unique in man. Neither brutes nor pure spirits suffer shame. Man's place in nature can be accurately determined by a study of the role that shame plays in his life-spirit composite. Shame, in turn, is related to a number of other emotional responses closely linked to man's social nature.[2]

From references in *Formalism* we know that Scheler's study on shame was completed as early as 1913. As late as 1921 he hoped to include this essay among his studies on the emotional life. But as we have seen, the series of works on the meaning of the emotions and their laws was never published.[3] As a result, Scheler's essay, "On Shame and the Feeling of Shame," was first published among the *Posthumous Writings* of 1933.[4]

Again, the meaning and use of terms becomes a problem. To translate Scheler's term, *Scham*, into its immediate English equivalent, *shame*, is far too simple (though in identifying titles there is little alternative). In English, *shame* connotes too much the meaning of guilt. The term, a *sense of modesty*, as used in discussions of chastity, comes very close to Scheler's meaning of *Scham*. But *modesty*, then, is a virtue, part of the larger virtue of temperance, and does not refer directly to the primitive emotional response of Scheler's discussion. Furthermore, a *modest* man in English more generally means an unpretentious man. For Scheler, *Scham* refers to both a bodily and a spiritual emotional embarrassment. Such a generic emotional response can be described as "a defensive feeling of one's self-integrity."

---

[1] Ch. X of Part One, only two pages, treats of "The Moral Value of Fellow-Feeling," *Sympathie*, 151–52; *Sympathy*, 138–39.

[2] *Nachlass*, 68, 76–77.

[3] Cf. *supra*, Ch. III.

[4] Cf. "Bemerkungen zu den Manuskripten," *Nachlass*, 510–11, for bibliographical and textual details. This essay takes up eighty pages of *Nachlass*, 65–147, with another seven additional pages of "Zusätze" added by the editor from other Schelerian manuscripts.

The most essential element of the shame-experience is the reflective awareness of one's own individual self-identity, either in his bodily characteristics or as a person. One feels himself to be an individualized instance within a general situation.[1] Thus a child before its parents, a wife before her husband or a model before an artist feels no self-embarrassment unless and until, through some deliberate or indeliberate act, the individual is made to feel that his (or her) individual self, in all its individual bodily parts, is under direct scrutiny. There is no feeling of shame as long as one loses himself within the immediacy of the present, living situation; e.g., a husband and wife together. There is no feeling of shame as long as one considers himself as part of a general class; e.g., as long as the model is a general model and not *this* model. But at the very moment of withdrawal from the situational moment, one is not only directly conscious of himself, but he suffers emotionally some feeling, some sense of the need to protect his own self-integrity. This can happen to one who is entirely alone; this can happen to one at the higher level of the spiritual person. Scheler's study of this feeling is directed to an understanding of its expressional, symbolic meaning, not its empirical causes or its goal.

The first (lower) form of the sense of shame is that associated with the body and its parts at the vitalistic level of the basic life impulses. This is the sense (or feeling) of one's own physical self-integrity. The emotional responses here center around the sex organs and their proper covering.[2] While sexuality is one of the primary instances of shame, it is not in itself the origin or cause of shame nor the most basic element in the understanding of the expressionable meaning of shame.

Traditions and customs control and modify the modes (*Arten*) of the external occasions of shame, but they do not effect the basic emotion itself. Thus, the use of clothes is only one social reaction to the sense of shame, but by no means the only one. Primitives may be unclothed, but not "naked," not "ashamed"—unless the shame arises from another source. Only certain types of cultures associate "being unclothed" with nakedness and shame.[3] A sense of shame and modesty is as much a part

---

[1] Dupuy, *op. cit.*, 29–30, points out that this notion of shame was already elaborated upon by Scheler in *Logical and Ethical Principles* of 1897.

[2] The easy association of shame with sex is very natural in German, since many of the common terms for the genitalia are compounded with *Scham*. The term *privates* contains some of the meaning of the individuality of sexuality.

[3] *Nachlass*, 75. Scheler said that, when a man wears a nightshirt to bed, that man considers nakedness to be more in the disrobing of his clothes than considering clothes as the covering for his nakedness.

of the essential emotional make-up of a man as it is of a woman, but the degree of intensity of the emotion is greater with the woman.[1] These are but a few of the insights that Scheler expounded as belonging to the essence of shame.

The second form of a sense of self-integrity (of shame) is at the mental or spiritual level (*Seelenscham oder das geistige Schamgefühl*). This is not merely the result of education. It is a primary experience. But neither is it the sole source of morality. In so far as education may control the external occasions of shame (which is something very different from the genuine feeling itself), the sense of shame tends to be converted into *prudery*. The prude is excessively concerned about the projected purpose (*Zweck*) of his "purity" and about its external execution. The "pure and modest man," with a proper sense of shame, experiences the intrinsic ends (*Ziele*) of the feeling and automatically and spontaneously performs "pure" actions in all their full integrity.[2]

A number of other positive personal responses are closely associated with a "spiritual sense of shame." These include the sense of awe and reverence and the virtue of humility. A person finds himself within all of life, or before other persons, or before God, and, conscious of the fact that other values exist outside of and independent from himself, he withdraws with a fearful respect.[3] Present in this experience is the element essential to all shame: the reflective look upon oneself as being distinct from the universal generality of things. Of course, the opposite moral response is possible. In this case, having considered his own Self in relation to the totality of things, a person becomes vain and proud of his own individuality.

At this point, it is not possible to make a complete study of Scheler's theory of virtues.[4] We only want to understand this theory within the context of man's place in the metaphysics of life and spirit. Virtues (and moral values) do not arise originally and exclusively from the social factors in man's nature. Paradoxically, their origin is understood by the fact that man experiences himself as non-social, as an individual within life and among other persons, but as having some relation to the rest of life and to other persons. Virtues, like values, are originally individual: they pre-suppose man's awareness of his own self-integrity.

---

[1] *Nachlass*, 145–47.
[2] *Nachlass*, 93.
[3] *Nachlass*, 88–90.
[4] The complete study of Scheler's anthropology would include the study of the virtues. A fine essay on humility and reverence is "Towards the Rehabilitation of Virtue," *Umsturz*, 13–31.

This consciousness is nothing more than a general feeling of "shame."

LOVE

Love at its highest level is a distinct experience-act between persons. Our study of Scheler's theory of love will proceed in three stages. First, we will study how this theory has inter-connections within the body of his thought. Then the relations between love and sympathy and the naturalistic theories of love will be examined. Finally, the unique value and dignity of love in human life will be studied.

Scheler's theory of love agreed with his philosophy of man, his general metaphysics and with his ethical theory concerning intrinsic "material" values. Affective responses are made to values given within the emotional experience. Love is an act that is directed not to values. Primarily, human love, when it is moral love, is directed to the *person* of the other.

Scheler distinguished various *forms* of love. These forms of love corresponded to the fourfold hierarchy of values which he had delineated in *Formalism*. The lowest values are the sensory feelings of the pleasant and the unpleasant. Scheler declared that there could be no genuine *love* of the merely pleasant: we cannot really "love apple pie." The affective response to sense pleasures gives evidence of some feeling or interest in the sensibly pleasant object, but there is no desire to have the bearer of values fulfill its own higher potentialities. Feelings of pleasantness may accompany some forms of love. But if these feelings begin to dominate, love diappears and the *pleasant* merely becomes a means to our own self-satisfaction.

Vital or passionate love, corresponding to the vital values of health, vigor and nobility, is the first instance of real love. Sexual love, love of the noble, authentic friendship, married love and love within the family are examples of vital love. Vital love is the bond of union within life-community. Scheler's respect for life and for all living things led him to declare that living things are real bearers of values and, as such, deserve our respectful consideration—our love. To abuse living things is evil in itself without any further reference to man or to persons. Man's love and reverence for his own body has its source in vital love. Sexual love, another type of vital love, is not a mere response to sensible pleasure; as we have seen, Scheler's lengthy discourses on the sexual act was to emphasize its role in man's vital union with the totality of life-processes.[1]

Spiritual values include aesthetic values, the juridical values of the just and the unjust, and pure knowledge. Corresponding to the spiritual values is *mental love (die seelische Liebe)*. Mental love results in intellectual ties, in cultural and educational relationships. Mental love is the bond of union in society.

The fourth and highest type of values in the scale of values are the religious values of the holy and the unholy which effect such responses as bliss, awe and worship. Corresponding to this class of values is the *spiritual love of persons* which is a strictly moral love between persons. Personal love, a sense of moral solidarity and the knowledge of common salvation is the bond of unity in the person-community.

Between men there can be present all the forms of love: personal love, mental love and vital love (and also a sensible, passionate attraction by way of sense pleasure). These loves can be present in a number of ways. I can have close intellectual ties (mental love) with someone who is physically repulsive to me and at the same time I can have (or have not) personal love for him. A common plight of the artist (as depicted) is to fall in real passionate love with someone who is degrading to him both in mind and in person. Scheler maintained that these forms of love are essentially separable, despite the fact that in actuality they usually occur together. The same term *love* is used to designate all three forms of love.

Moral love in the full sense of the term is related immediately to the value of the person as such. Personal love is directed immediately to the other concrete individual person. Here, again, Scheler's theory on the individuation of persons is paramount. The other person whom we encounter is irreducible to anything else except as being himself an absolute, ultimate concrete center of spiritual acts. Our love for him goes out exclusively to his unique person. Love of persons is not only the highest love, but it is the basis and the model of all other forms of love. Love of persons is the primary instance of love, and, as it were, the primary analogate for all our other discussions of love. It is on this basis that Scheler distinguished love from sympathy and from all naturalistic explanation of love.

First of all, Scheler distinguished love from benevolence, especially from that benevolence based upon pity. Benevolence in this sense in-

---

[1] Much of the essay on shame and most of Ch. VII in Part Two in *Sympathy* is discussion of the full meaning of the sexual act.

volves our exerting ourselves for the material benefit of others, our wishing others well, as we stand a distance above them. Through our good works we become satisfied with our neighbor's improved welfare. Love, however, is an act that springs spontaneously between persons. Love is directed to the very person of the other. While our neighbor's material welfare may be improved, it is his very spiritual person that is the subject of our love.

Scheler's phenomenological analysis of love dealt immediately with the concrete acts of love-experiencings. Therefore, love is no mere disposition or tendency or habit; love is no abstract theoretical principle associated with a universal finality. It is defined in its essence as an *act* or *movement*. It is a spontaneous movement, with a necessary reference to values, but the motion of love is directed to the *bearer* of values and not to the values themselves. A love-act is so directed to the value-bearing subject that that subject may obtain the highest possible values suitable to its nature. Thus, if I love a plant, an animal or a person, I desire for that individual thing the highest ideal values compatible with it. This is the meaning of Scheler's formal definition of love.

Love is that movement in which every concrete individual object which is a bearer of values successfully achieves the highest values possible for that object according to its ideal determination. Again, [love is that movement] in which it [a concrete individual subject] attains the ideal value-essence proper to it.[1]

Hatred, of course, is an act diametrically opposed to love, but identical with love in its intrinsic act-essence. Hatred is not directed to non-values (I do not properly hate a person's vulgarity) but to the bearer of values (I hate the person himself). In love, I love a person with or without high values—I love him so that in my loving him he can achieve the higher values. So also, in hatred, I hate a person with or without values, but I hate him to despoil him of his values. If a person be vulgar or noble, I can either love him or hate him.

Scheler completely rejected the common aphorism that love is blind. Love is not blind: it instills vision and knowledge where otherwise they are lacking. If a man seems such that only his mother could love him, his mother has *real love* for him only because she sees in him the dignity of a person who does possess or can possess the highest of values. Only love can produce such knowledge. A Christian loves the weak and the

---

[1] (Our own translation.) "Liebe ist die Bewegung, in der jeder konkret individuelle Gegenstand, der Werte trägt, zu den für ihn und nach seiner Bestimmung möglichen höchsten Werten gelangt; oder in der er sein ideales Wertwesen, das ihm eigentümlich ist, erreicht." *Sympathie*, 174; cf. *Sympathy*, 161.

poor, not out of pity or motives of *ressentiment*, but because he sees that each person is capable of new and higher types of values.

Scheler's definition of love as an *act* must be taken very strictly according to his distinction between *act* and *function*. *Act* belongs exclusively within the realm of the spiritual and the personal: it is not a composite *function* of the *I*-body or the self.[1] This, then, sharply distinguishes love from fellow-feeling. Love is a *spontaneous act*; sympathy is a *responsive function*. Sympathy involves an affective reaction to another *I*: it is, literally, a *feeling*-with the other *I*. In German, and especially in English, vocabulary begins to falter. Feelings (*Gefühle*) and affections (*Affekte*) in this context refer only to those human activities that necessarily involve the responsive resonance of the body. Love as a spiritual act is a "movement of the heart," a "spiritual emotion." Scheler was satisfied to include *love* within the generic term *Gemütsbewegung*, but the normal English translation for this term as *emotion* would not resolve the ambiguity. "Love is a movement of the heart and a spiritual act." (*Liebe ist eine Bewegung des Gemüts und ein geistiger Akt*).[2] This is Scheler's statement, and his meaning is clear, but we grope for words to express it. The scholastic meaning of *appetite* and *appetition* can be employed in this generic sense, so that we can speak meaningfully of a "spiritual act of appetition." This would convey Scheler's thought fairly well, but in a vocabulary far removed from his. Most words are contrived to convey strictly cognitive meaning. It is difficult to define and describe such non-cognitive acts as acts of love, acts of reverence, of beauty-appreciation, etc., all of which belong essentially to the core of person.

Love and fellow-feeling complement each other in a number of ways. Fellow-feeling is based upon love and varies according to the measure and depth of our love. Therefore, our sympathy is nobler and of greater ethical significance if it is feeling based upon vital, mental or spiritual love. As a matter of fact, we can sympathize with an individual we do not love, but even in this case our sympathy rests essentially upon love, but upon a more generic love, i.e., we love this man's family, his country, the human race. If we love some one, we will necessarily feel sympathy for him. We cannot have hatred and sympathy towards the same person.

On the other hand, if we sympathize with someone, especially if we "feel sorry with" (*Mitleid*) someone, without loving that person, we

[1] Cf. *supra*, Ch. II.
[2] *Sympathie*, 154; cf. *Sympathy*, 142.

insult him, we shame him and humiliate him. Nietzsche was correct
when he spoke out against a loveless pity. Schopenhauer and others who
try to construct a theory of love based upon pity were surely wrong.
All forms of humanitarianism teach a love for mankind, but a pure
philanthropist has only *pity* for the individual instances of real people.[1]
In the 1913 essay of *Ressentiment*, Scheler struck out against the subversion of values that this attitude entailed.[2] His 1917 address, "Christian Love and the Twentieth Century," continued the defense of love
against its false counterfeits.[3]

Among the naturalistic theories of love, Scheler classified these four.
1) Those theories that base sympathy upon imitation, reproduction and
empathy, and, by way of benevolence, derive love from sympathy.
2) The phylogenetic and positivistic theories that explain sympathy by
reference to the social instinct and impulse. 3) Theories based upon
a special philosophy of history. 4) Freud's then recent ontogenetic
theory of love which Scheler understood as holding love to derived
wholly from sexuality. Scheler considered Freud's contribution to be
the main buttress supporting all the other naturalistic theories of love.[4]

Much of Scheler's critique employed against the genetic theories of
sympathy could be applied here, for many of these theories of love were
based upon a theory of sympathy. Very characteristically, Scheler refused to reduce the purely spiritual phenomenon of personal love to
mere naturalistic, vital instincts. Naturalists remain blind to values of a
personal and sacred love that transcend their own realm. "Sublimation"
can have no meaning unless a realm of higher values is posited antecedent to, and independent from, the vital instincts themselves. The
"theories of transference," by which the same lower love-instincts are
directed to a number of successive objects, fail again to perceive the
essentially spiritual aspects of love, the various forms of love and how
the act of love in the first instance is necessarily directed exclusively to
a single subject.[5]

Scheler vigorously defended the essential transcendence of love as a

[1] The last chapter (Ch. XI) of Part One of *Sympathy*, "The Relationship of Love and Fellow-Feeling," is a transition to Part Two, on Love and Hatred. *Sympathie*, 152–57; *Sympathy*,
140–44.
[2] *Umsturz*, 33–147. It is this essay that is published in the English translation as *Ressentiment*.
[3] *Ewigen*, 357–401; *Eternal*, 357–402.
[4] Cf. Ch. V. of Part Two of *Sympathy*, "The Limitations of the Naturalistic Theory of
Love." *Sympathie*, 188–92; *Sympathy*, 175–79.
[5] Cf. the greater part of Ch. VI of Part Two of *Sympathy* for Scheler's critique of the naturalistic theories of love. *Sympathy*, 192–227; *Sympathy*, 180–209. Here, again, is revealed
Scheler's own understanding of Freud.

spiritual act and its pre-eminent dignity in its personal and moral
dimensions. Interpersonal love takes on a still deeper dimension in so
far as it touches upon the holy and the sacred. Love that is directed to
another person is in confrontation with an ultimate, irreducible factor,
an absolute—and the *absolute* is one of the qualities of the *holy*. Person
cannot be objectified in knowledge. No more can person be objectified
in love. The purely moral value of a person can be "known" in the
ultimate sense only by the act by which we love him. Love gives understanding. It is not the scholar or the theoretical theologian who know
the moral worth of the person of Christ, but His loving disciple who
walks in his Master's footsteps.[1]

Man's love of God is love directed to a person, the Person of Persons.
Therefore, this love does not follow a conceptualization of God, nor is it
a benevolent love *for* God (as if we could improve God's welfare). Our
love of God participates in, is co-executive with (*Mitvollzug*), God's own
love of the world and His love of Himself. Only in the loving of God
do we begin to understand the meaning of His infinite essence which is
Love. At this point, Scheler introduced the phrases of mystic theology:
amare mundum in Deo, amare Deum in Deo, or simply, *amare in Deo*. For
him, these phrases describe the full reality of things.[2]

The religious dimension of man is not a mere epiphenomenon or a
late evolutionary development. In the very core of their being, all
finite persons necessarily are oriented towards God. In God, each
finite person is to realize the ideal of his own eternal vocation. Nor is
this the sole concern of the individual. In God we become conscious of a
common unity among all persons for salvation (*Heilssolidäritätsbewusst-
sein*). "The individual responsibility of persons stands or falls *along with*
their collective responsibility (which they have from the beginning and
cannot spontaneously assume)."[3] "To love in God" effects a non-
cosmic love of persons in a manner the Oriental mystics never attained.
By "loving in God," the Christian can love all men individually and
collectively, but without the cold universality of humanitarian benevo-

---

[1] *Sympathie*, 180–81; *Sympathy*, 167–68. Erich Fromm, in *The Art of Loving: An Inquiry into
the Nature of Love* (New York: Harper Colophon Books, 1962) reveals many close ties with
Scheler's theory of love. Martin D'Arcy, S.J., in *The Mind and Heart of Love* (New York:
Meridian Books, 1956) devotes a whole chapter (Ch. IX, 231–262) to "Love and Sympathy."
He identifies the two principles of anima and animus (key terms in his whole exposition of
love) with Scheler's life and spirit. D'Arcy's short descriptions of Scheler's theories are good
and his critical reactions are sound.
[2] *Sympathie*, 177–78; *Sympathy*, 164–65.
[3] *Sympathy*, 129. "Selbstverantwortlichkeit und ursprüngliche (nicht erst frei selbstverant-
wortlich übernommene) Mitverantwortlichkeit der Person stehen eben und fallen *zusammen*."
Sympathie, 143.

lence. Through this "love in God" there results the principle for the solidarity of all moral being, a moral love between persons, which is the basis for *person-community*.[1]

PERSON-COMMUNITY

Scheler's theory of person-community is the capstone of his philosophy of man and of person. One explicit discussion on community appeared in *Eternal*, in the address "Christian Love and the Twentieth Century." This address was delivered in 1917; it synthesized many isolated discussions on community scattered through *Formalism, Sympathy* and *Ressentiment*.

Scheler's study of person-community was, of course, a phenomenological investigation. He sought to know the essence (*Wesen*) of person-community and its intrinsic ends (*Ziele*). The eternal, ideal essence of a rational person includes not only that person's self-conscious responsibility for himself, but also his co-responsibility for and with others in so far as they *are, live* and *act* together as members of person-community. All possible finite spiritual beings (includings the angels and the souls of the dead) by their essence are members of this community.

There is a consciousness of community-membership, a "spiritual intention" (*geistige Intention*) directed towards community, independently of the contingent fact whether a man actually lives in community or is a solitary recluse. Robinson Crusoe is the recurring example of a man without actual fellows, but who remains essentially a community-being. In other words the definition of man as a social animal (Aristotle's "political animal") is not gained by a historical, sociological or evolutionary study. Through a series of phenomenological reductions, the full meaning of man, in the sense of transcendental psychology, is that the essence of man includes man's intentional-community-orientation. "*As certainly as I am is there a 'we,'* or I *belong* to a 'we.'"[2]

Therefore, man is not a communal being only in reference to his body-animal nature. The many facts of physical birth, of infantile helplessness, of the two sexes and of various gregarious instincts support this obvious truth. But man is a member of community also in his rational and spiritual nature.

[1] *Sympathie*, 178; *Sympathy*, 165.
[2] *Eternal*, 373–74. "*So wahr Ich bin, so wahr sind wir*, oder *gehöre* ich zu einem 'wir'." *Ewigen*, 371–72.

The spiritual and personal community of man exists in its own right and in its own origin. In both right and origin it is superior to the biological community.[1]

Scheler defended the transcendence of spiritual community by employing the same line of argument which he used in defending the whole realm of spirit as irreducible to the lower levels of being.

Scheler contined the phenomenological investigation of man's consciousness of his membership in person-community. This consciousness does not depend upon our concrete historical circumstances. Furthermore, the more we consider the visible communities to which we belong (family, city, nation, circle of friends), the more we come to understand that not one of these earthly communities can ever satisfy the full demands of our reason and heart for a more perfect spiritual-personal community. In this yearning there is a supreme kind of love of God, long before we conceive of the idea of God. Scheler accepted this "sociological proof for God" as genuine evidence (*Erweis*) for God's existence. The evidence here, rising exclusively from our idea of the community of personal, spiritual beings, is original evidence, independent from other proofs, but it leads to the same intrinsic end (*Ziel*) in its discovery of God.[2]

The community-experience of persons leads them to the knowledge of the perfect community they experience in their relation to the Person of God. Not only is this the real matter of the case, but Scheler made the next step. All community-experience is incomplete until it is had within the background consciousness of God, in Whom the supreme and final community of all spiritual beings receive its fulfillment. "It is in and through *God* that for the first time we are truly *bound in spirit* to one another."[3]

It is this principle that functions in many key parts of *Sympathy* and through all of *Ressentiment*. This is the case of *amare in Deo* as applied to personal community. Persons love one another fully to the extent that their love is orientated to their common locus in the Godhead. It is here that we become conscious of a common salvation. It is here that a non-cosmic love of persons is first possible. Christian love is the perfect embodiment of such a real love of concrete individual persons, because in each person we recognize our fellowship with him in God.

---

[1] *Eternal*, 374. "Des Menschen Geistes – und Persongemeinschaft ist vielmehr eigenen und höheren Rechts und eigenen, und zwar höheren Ursprungs als diese 'Lebensgemeinschaft'." *Ewigen*, 373.

[2] *Ewigen*, 373–74; *Eternal*, 375–76.

[3] *Eternal*, 375. "In Ihm und durch Ihn sind wir wahrhaftig *geistig* auch erst unter uns verbunden." *Ewigen*, 374.

Such a line of reasoning was by no means an empty piece of senti-
mental moralizing for Scheler. That persons possess a mutual community-consciousness in God was an integral part of his metaphysics.
His theory for the individuation of persons left itself open to the attack
that this was a theory of absolute metaphysical individualism, in which
each person is a type of Leibnizian monad, complete in itself. On the
other hand, strict vitalism and forms of Oriental pantheism taught a
pure monism, in which the individual persons lost all concrete sub-
stantiality (*Daseinssubstantialität der geistigen Person*). Scheler's theory of
sympathy and of love retained both elements: the individuality of
persons but a mutual living together between them. His theory of
personal community bases man's ultimate community-consciousness
upon the essential metaphysical union between all individual persons
in the Person of God.[1]

One aspect of this communal unity which we have already seen is the
sense of collective responsibility men feel for one another and for their
whole social group. Individually, man is responsible for his own
vocation which he finds only in God. But, further, man's sense of
community in God makes him originally responsible for all men.
Collective responsibility carries with it a sense of collective guilt. We
feel ourselves truly co-responsible before God for the entire moral and
religious condition of the collective moral group.[2]

The world of finite moral persons rests upon an intrinsic solidary
unity which Scheler called "the principle of solidarity." In *Formalism*,
Scheler declared that the most basic unifying principle of the *Gesamtperson* (of all finite persons) is this intrinsic moral-religious bond of unity
which all persons feel towards one another. The principle of moral
solidarity among persons is an essential and *a priori* factor of all personal
relatedness in community.[3]

For Scheler, person-community serves as the fundamental basis for
all later social relations. The various political theories of social contract, the social-economic schemes of classes, guilds and estates, the
religious theories concerning man's relationship to God, are so many
instances of empty theorizing if they do not accept the original communal nature of man. Theories of man's radical individualism fail totally
to account for man's social nature.

Moral solidarity of finite persons in community becomes for Scheler,

[1] *Sympathie*, 142–43; *Sympathy*, 128–29.
[2] *Ewigen*, 373–75; *Eternal*, 376–77.
[3] *Formalismus*, 537–40.

in his phenomenological investigation, a basic principle arrived at through natural reason. But in his theistic-Catholic period, he also declared that this became the fundamental idea for the Christian teaching of original sin, of collective redemption in Christ and of the unity of the people of God in the Church as members of Christ's body.[1]

Scheler's study of the social emotions of sympathy, shame and love found its fulfillment in his description of personal love through moral solidarity in person-community. Person-community transcends the purely biological and vitalistic community. But neither is it the bare intellectual association of society. All the best elements of spirit, in its transcendence and in its affective involvement in being and salvation, are included in Scheler's theory of person-community.

---

[1] *Ewigen*, 377; *Eternal*, 378. Perhaps the most obvious cases where Scheler's thoughts have been incorporated within the thought of a Catholic theologian are the two small works of Guardini, *Vom Sinn der Kirche* (Mainz: Matthias-Grünewald, 1933) and *Vom Geist der Liturgie* (Freiburg im Breisgau: Herder, 1934). These two works were translated as one volume, *The Church and the Catholic and the Spirit of the Liturgy* (New York: Sheed & Ward, 1940).

CHAPTER SIX

CONCLUSION

Because of the diffuseness of Scheler's work and the shifts of thought during his lifetime, a simple schema of his thought is highly problematic at best. Yet it is instructive to attempt to give as systematized a schema as possible of some of the fundamental principles functioning throughout Scheler's works. This not only gives us a working summary of much of his thought, but also allows us to add a number of reflective and critical comments.

ATTEMPTED SYNTHESIS

Most of Scheler's writings are diffuse both in style and in content. At times, however, he attempted in a few brief strokes to unite and outline vast amounts of material in a few simple schemata. At first sight, it would seem that most of these schemata coincided with and complemented one another. But upon closer investigation, many difficulties arise. Scheler himself must have known that some of these brief outlines could not be easily reconciled with one another.

One of the most fundamental and lasting principles in all of Scheler's thought is his contention that values are immediately given in an objective, permanent, hierarchical scale. This teaching from *Formalism* underwent no appreciable change throughout his life. The scale of values was fourfold, ranking from the lowest to the highest.

1. Sensory feelings of the pleasant and the unpleasant and of the useful.
2. Vital values—health, vigor, nobility.
3. Spiritual values.
   a. aesthetic values.
   b. juridical values of just and unjust,
   c. pure knowledge.
4. Religious values of the holy and the unholy. Bliss, awe, worship.

According to Scheler's metaphysics, the two attributes of being are the vital impulse (*Drang*) and spirit (*Geist*), the real and ideal factors of being. The two lower values (the pleasant and vital values) are reducible to the life-impulse; the phenomena of spirit arise with the two higher values (the spiritual and religious values).

In *Sympathy* Scheler defined the four forms of love according to this same hierarchy of values.

1. No genuine "love" of the pleasant. A mere affective response to value: a feeling or interest.
2. Vital or passionate love. Sexual love. Love of the noble, friendship, marriage, family.
3. Mental love. Intellectual ties. Cultural and educational relationships.
4. Spiritual love of persons. Only love of persons is moral love.

This is parallel with the four forms of social life.

1. Herd or Mass. United by emotional infection and unconscious and unwilling following.
2. Life-community. A conscious living and feeling together. A natural unity, achieving spontaneously the goals of the group.
3. Society. An artificial, deliberate and purposefully constructed group, with laws and statements of its goals. Individuals create society by contracts and laws.
4. Person-community. Collective person. Moral solidarity under God. Co-responsibility, co-merit, co-guilt.

In the study on shame in 1913, Scheler made a similar division of the forms of shame.

1. There is no form of shame at the inorganic level.
2. Feeling of shame over one's own physical self-integrity, over one's own body and sexual organs.
3. Feeling of self-integrity at the mental or spiritual level. Feeling of intellectual inferiority before experts.
4. Personal or spiritual sense of shame—awe, reverence and humility —before values, being, God and other persons.

Also in *Models and Leaders*, written at about the same time, Scheler made a fourfold division of ideal types of persons.

1. The Producer, the Provider, who makes things pleasant for life or directs to what is useful for life.
2. Hero, protector of noble values.
3. The Genius, holding high spiritual values.
4. The Holy Person, the founder of religion, the saint.

These five schemata all appear in the early works of Scheler and quite simply complement one another. However, they all contain the slightly

ambiguous division between spiritual values and religious values. At the
level of spiritual values (mental love, society, the genius) there occur
phenomena that are genuine expressions of spirit, but which seem to
lack all affective and emotional dimensions. We saw this ambiguity in
Scheler's definition of philosophy. If philosophy is a purely mental,
intellectual activity, it is not yet a totally personal involvement in being,
it is not yet the activity of a full person.

In *Man's Place*, a late work, Scheler made this simple division.
1. The inorganic.
2. The organic.
3. The sentient: sensation and consciousness.
4. The person.

The basic drive (*Drang*) exists at the inorganic level as unorganized
within centers of atomic energy. Only at the organic level is there an
inner being, a for-and-in-themselves being (*ein Fürsich- und Innesein*),
where the common vital impulse (*Gefühlsdrang*) occurs. Man participates in this biological drive towards growth and reproduction at the
vegetative level of his being. At the sentient level occur instincts, habits
(through association and conditioned reflex) and practical intelligence.
Brute animals are capable of these activities, and, therefore, this class
of phenomena is not to be ascribed to spirit. With spirit there is the
intellectual objectification of reality and a consciousness of Self. The
center of spiritual acts is the Person.

At this point, Scheler's clearly defined categories tend to disintegrate.
Another division of the phenomena within man occurs in *Man's Place*'
1. The inorganic. Man's participation in the chemical and physical
   properties of material things.
2. The organic. Man's vegetative, biological life.
3. The *I*, the body-*I*, the experienced *I*. The *I* functions as intrinsically and essentially related to body-*I*-experiences.
4. Person. Center of spiritual acts. Can objectify reality and have
   consciousness of the *I*. *Acts* occur here which transcend body-
   space-time dimensions. Also affective acts such as love, bliss, awe.

This last schema cannot be simply super-imposed upon the former
ones. The body-*I*, as such, is not the source of spiritual values, of mental
love, or that which is guided by genius. Yet, there is a sense in which
the person of *man* (as distinct from that of the angels or of God) con-
fronts his own Self and his fellow spirit-in-body-men only at the body-*I*
level. All the difficulties in understanding Scheler's doctrine on spirit,
person and *I* meet at this point, along with his definitions of philosophy,

metaphysics and the salvational knowledge of religion. It may be asked whether Scheler ever successfully resolved the difficulties of a Cartesian dualism, of a Kantian phenomenal self and noumenal soul, by all his maneuvering. These difficulties were inherent in Scheler's thought and remained unresolved at the end.

CRITICAL SUMMARY

Scheler's personality was injected into his thought, not only during his life, but also by his students after his death. A study of his personality is a necessary part of the study of his thought. Nevertheless, the controlled, critical study of his writings reveals a strong line of inner consistency and strength. If his late meta-anthropological pantheism seems to be an extreme position, it was well prepared for by his early choice of principles and methodology in philosophy.

Similar to most phenomenologists, Scheler was pre-occupied with genuine metaphysical questions. He ascribed to being the two irreducible attributes of *life* and *spirit*. For Scheler, these metaphysical questions were centered in the problem of man, but difficulties remain both at the level of metaphysics and as applied to man.

The most crucial metaphysical point for Scheler to demonstrate is that spirit is essentially different from and irreducible to life. His dialectics, however, seem to break down. While spirit should possess only ideal intellectuality, yet within the dialectics it too become active; it "opposes" life, it "contradicts" life. In spite of his own principles, Scheler introduced the language of life to describe spirit. Indeed, if there is any *activity* of spirit it must be described in vitalistic terms. But how is spirit to *love*, to respond to religious values, to form a spiritual community? Scheler's metaphysics becomes a limping dualism, for life alone bears the greater portion of being. Not only is spirit's presence in man suspect, but the Deity itself becomes absorbed into the lower life processes. An evolving, unfinished God can hardly serve as the object of authentic religious experience.

In man, the dual principles of life and spirit tend to destroy the very unity that Scheler wished to define and to defend. Man himself becomes bifurcated in and through these two dualistic principles. The final unity of man in his person-*I*, person-body-*I* relationship remains open to question.

Scheler took up the traditional phenomenological attack against psychologism in setting forth his theories of sympathy and of man's knowledge of other men. He sought to *understand* the *meaningfulness* of man's social emotions, rather than to *explain* these emotions scientifically in their causal genesis. According to Scheler, our primary awareness of others is an originary given of consciousness; the world of the communal "we" is essentially given prior to the knowledge of my own individualized Self or the knowledge of other contingent factual *I*'s. This is a bold and refreshing answer to the question concerning the perception of others. Variations of such a theory are being accepted today by some psychologists, as well as by many phenomenologists.

In principle, according to Scheler, person and its spiritual acts cannot be objectified in knowledge. A knowledge of and a living together with other persons is achieved only by participating in the being of the other person by co-achieving, pre-performing and re-executing our own spiritual acts alongside those of the alien person in person-community. The non-objectifiable character of person is a particularly valuable and influential contribution by Scheler to contemporary thought.

Scheler's phenomenology also led to studies in sociology where his formulation of the sociology of knowledge became very influential. He described four forms of sociality (the mass, life-community, society and person-community) in an attempt to synthesize his dualistic metaphysical principles of life and spirit into a social anthropology. This division is somewhat contrived and artificial; the individually divided categories are extremely difficult to verify.

Scheler's study on sympathy remains a genuinely worthwhile contribution to our knowledge of man. His theories of love and shame are not only consistent with his own thought, but also reveal some fine insights into the understanding of these social feelings. His description of person-community is a gallant effort at synthesizing all the better elements of life and spirit, of intellect and heart, of knowledge and love between finite persons and with God, the Person of Persons. Nevertheless, the theory speaks more from the heart than from the mind; it is more of a wish conjecture, than a philosophical description of reality. Surely one must question the ontological status of such a "collective person" (*Gesamtperson*). One wonders if Scheler seriously proposed to show that the unity of all the spiritual acts in a person-community was such that they constituted a *real person*. In what way is such a collective person in its unified constitution analogous to the unified constitution of a single person? If Scheler held both types of persons to possess an identical ontological status, one wonders all the more about the final study and metaphysical ground for person itself.

FINAL COMMENTS ON COMMUNITY

Scheler's study of community is a phenomenological study of the very essence of community, to discover its essential forms and intrinsic ends. The community most proper to man is person-community, which results from the essential activity of spirit in man. It is inherent in the eternal, ideal essence of man that he is outwardly conscious of community relations to others. According to Scheler, man's intentional relatedness to others is more fundamental, is a more originary given datum of consciousness, than the knowledge of his own individuality. Therefore, the "we" of community is prior to my individual "*I*". This description of person-community is made independently from all considerations of man's biological needs, his evolutionary origins, or his factual, historical situation. As *spirit* is essentially superior to and independent of *life*, so is person-community above and free from life-community.

Person-community finds its fulfillment in the Person of God. It is in and through God that for the first time we are truly bound in spirit to one another. Here is the source of the principle of moral solidarity, the principle that we live together in community through reciprocal moral-religious obligations towards one another, as well as a co-responsibility for the moral good of the whole collective group before God. There is a reciprocity of love between persons, according to Scheler's theory of love, wherein there is not love *for* another person as an object of knowledge, but in loving another we participate in the being of another. In this way, all finite persons in community participate in the being of God. This is a primary application of Augustine's phrase, so loved by Scheler, that we are to love the world and to love one another "in God" (*amare mundum in Deo*).

One question forcibly presents itself. Scheler's theory of community was devised during his early Catholic period. It has explicit dependence upon Christian faith in creation and redemption and, in the very least, was based upon theistic principles. Scheler's late development in metaphysics denied theism in favor of the idea of a meta-anthropological emergence of the Deity. How did this new theory of God-becoming-God-in-man affect Scheler's theory of community?

Scheler himself, of course, did not live to re-work all his earlier philosophy into the schema of his new metaphysics. He published no later views on community explicitly. However, we have seen that his later metaphysical views had many earlier roots and that the development in thought was not nearly as revolutionary as it may seem. A careful re-study of this teaching of *amare in Deo* and the moral-religious solidarity of man in God may show that not only is this view compatible with an emergent God, but Scheler's early theory of community may have served as one of the stepping stones to a restatement of his whole meta-physics.

Man essentially is a religious animal. Religion is no late phenomenon in the natural evolution of man, but as soon as man is conscious of him-self, he is conscious of his dependence on God. Nor is the religious experience an exclusively individual experience. In its essence, it is originally a group experience: primitive tribes as a single person under-take the worship of their deities. This is simply another aspect of the solidarity principle, emphasizing the religious implications of our moral solidarity of the community in God. All religious phenomena are spiritual in essence. This is another concrete instance of the spirit transcending space-time material conditions and even the limitations of our own bodies. Scheler was propounding all this throughout his Catholic years. It would seem that, after 1923, Scheler would say that man's experience as a moral community in God is nothing more than one of the concrete instances where God begins to be realized within the living experiences of man.

A premature death cut short Scheler's lifelong search for God. Scheler has been called one of the "Great God-Searchers" of our time. In the words of St. Bernard, if God is so sweet to those who seek Him, what must He be to those who find Him!

BIBLIOGRAPHY OF PRIMARY SOURCES

The following is meant to be a near exhaustive list of the known extant writings by Max Scheler. A literal English translation of each work is immediately given and the time and place of the appearance and re-appearance of each work is carefully noted. Whenever English translations of Scheler's works have been published, these have been noted, but there is no notice given of translations into languages other than English.

Each volume of the carefully edited *Gesammelte Werke* of Max Scheler includes a rather complete list of Scheler's works, along with the pre-pared outline for their eventual complete publication in the *Gesammelte Werke*. The latest volumes of this set contain some minor corrections in the bibliography as Schelerian scholarship continues to perfect itself and as minor changes in the outline of publications occur. Noble (*Eternal, 457*) presented in English this incomplete version of Schelerian bibliography. Also, as an appendix to each volume, Maria Scheler, the general editor of the *Gesammelte Werke*, adds a long bio-bibliographical note to each of the individual articles. In 1963 Wilfried Hartmann (Stuttgart: Friedrich Fromann Verlag, 1963) published by far the most exhaustive list of books, articles and studies *by* Scheler, in trans-lation of Scheler, and *about* Scheler. The purpose of the present bibli-ography is to combine this information on the primary works of Scheler into summary form for English readers.

The following points explain the number-key in operation.

The works of Scheler are numbered according to the chronological order of their first publication.

The first number after the decimal refers to the particular edition of a certain work; e.g. 70.1 refers to the first edition of *Stellung*: 70.6 refers to its sixth edition.

The second number after the decimal has these meanings:

2 – the literal translation of the German title; e.g. 70.12 is a trans-lation of the title of the first edition of *Stellung*.

3 – our comment about the work; e.g. 70.13 is a comment about the first edition of *Stellung*: 70.63 would be a comment about the sixth edition. *4* – is a published English work; e.g. 70.64 is an English translation of the sixth edition of *Stellung* (and 70.643 is a comment about that translation). The third number (following a zero) refers to a part within the work; e.g. 74.201. This refers to a second edition of *Weltanschauung* and the *1* refers to the first article in this work. 74.2012 is its translation; 74.2013 is a comment on it. 74.202 refers to the second article and so on.

1.1	*Beiträge zur Feststellung der Beziehung zwischen den logischen und ethischen Prinzipien.* Jena: Vopelius, 1899. 142 pp.
1.12	Studies towards the Determination of the Relations between Logical and Ethical Principles.
1.13	Doctoral dissertation for the University of Jena in 1897.
2.1	"Arbeit und Ethik," *Zeitschrift für Philosophie und Philosophische Kritik*, 114 (1899), 161–200.
2.12	Work and Ethics.
2.13	First of several studies on work: see #62.20C3.
3.1	*Die transzendentale und die psychologische Methode.* Eine grundsätzliche Erörterung zur philosophischen Methodik. Jena: Dürr, 1900. 183 pp.
3.12	The Transcendental and Psychological Methods. A Basic Explanation for Philosophical Method.
3.13	*Habilitationsschrift* for the University of Jena in 1899.
3.2	Second, unrevised edition: Leipzig: Meiner, 1922.
4.1	"Kultur und Religion," *Der Wahrheitsgehalt der Religion.* Leipzig: Veit & Co., 1901.
4.12	Culture and Religion.
4.13	Work dedicated to Rudolf Eucken.
4.2	*Allgemeine Zeitung*, München, Beilage Nr. 30 (1903) 233–36.
5.1	"I. Kant und die moderne Kultur. Ein Gedenkblatt." *Allgemeine Zeitung*, München, Beilage Nr. 35 (1904) 273–80.
5.12	I. Kant and Modern Culture. A Dedication.

6.1   "Über Selbsttäuschungen," *Zeitschrift für Pathopsychologie* 1 (Heft 1), 87–163. Leipzig: Engelmann, 1911.

6.12   On Self-Delusions.

6.13   See #22.406, this essay was enlarged and retitled "Die Idole der Selbsterkenntnis"—"The Idols of Self-Knowledge"—and reprinted in *Umsturz*.

7.1   "Über Ressentiment und moralisches Werturteil. Ein Beitrag zur Pathologie der Kultur," *Zeitschrift für Pathopsychologie* 1 (Heft 2, 3), 268–368. Leipzig: Engelmann, 1912.

7.12   On *Ressentiment* and Moral Value-Judgement. A Study in the Pathology of Culture.

7.13   See #22.402. This work was enlarged and retitled "Das Ressentiment im Aufbau der Moralen"—"*Ressentiment* in the Construction of Morals"—and reprinted in *Umsturz*.

7.2   Special Printing. Leipzig: Engelmann, 1912. 103 pp.

7.24   M. Scheler, *Ressentiment*. Edited, with an Introduction by Lewis A. Coser. Translated by William A. Holdheim. New York: The Free Press of Glencoe, 1961. 201 pp.

7.243   This is a translation of the *Umsturz* article as it appeared in Band 3 of the *Gesammelte Werke*. It is admittedly a free translation, but faithful to the thought of Scheler.

8.1   *Zur Phänomenologie und Theorie der Sympathiegefühle und von Liebe und Hass.* Mit einem Anhang über den Grund zur Annahme der Existenz des fremden Ich. Halle: Niemeyer, 1913. 154 pp.

8.12   Towards the Phenomenology and Theory of the Feeling of Sympathy and on Love and Hatred. With an appendix concerning the basis for the assumption of the existence of the alien self.

8.13   See #61.2. This was enlarged under a new title in 1923.

9.1   "Der Formalismus in der Ethik und die materiale Wertethik. Mit besonderer Berücksichtigung der Ethik I. Kant." *Jahrbuch für Philosophie und phänomenologische Forschung.* Part One: volume One of *Jahrbuch*. Halle: Niemeyer, 1913, 405–565. Part Two: volume Two of *Jahrbuch*, 1916, 21–478.

9.12	Formalism in Ethics and Material Value-Ethics. With Special Reference to the Ethics of I. Kant." (The translation of *materiale* is highly contested.)
9.13	First edition of parts One and Two together, same title, with a Foreword. Halle: Niemeyer, 1916.
9.2	Second unrevised edition, with sub-title: "Neuer Versuch der Grundlegung eines ethischen Personalismus," and a second Foreword. Halle: Niemeyer, 1921.
9.22	New Attempt for the Foundation of an Ethical Personalism.
9.3	Third unrevised edition, with a third Foreword and an index. Halle: Niemeyer, 1927.
9.4	This work was the first to be published in the *Gesammelte Werke* (Band 2). It appeared as the fourth edition, based upon the second. M. Scheler, *Der Formalismus in der Ethik und die materiale Wertethik*. Neuer Versuch der Grundlegung eines ethischen Personalismus. Vierte durchgesehene Auflage. Herausgegeben mit einem neuen Sachregister von Maria Scheler. Bern: Francke, 1954. 676 pp.
9.43	This edition reprinted all three Forewords. Within its appendices it included a Postword by the editor, Maria Scheler (Scheler's wife), a list of textual emendations, a series of annotations and footnotes, a bibliography and a new index of topics and an index of persons. A similar set of appendices is included in each of the separate volumes of the *Gesammelte Werke*.
10.1	"Zur Funktion des geschlechtlichen Schamgefühles," *Geschlecht und Gesellschaft*, Berlin 8 (1913), 121–31, 177–90.
10.12	Concerning the Function of the Feeling of Sexual Shame.
10.13	This study was one of a series that was to appear in a separate work on the emotions. This book never appeared. See also #75.2023.
11.1	"Zur Psychologie der sogenannten Rentenhysterie," *Archiv für Sozialwissenschaften und Sozialpolitik*. Tübingen 37 (1913), 321–34.
11.12	The Psychology of the so-called Hysteria for Security.
11.13	Reprinted in *Umsturz* in slightly different form; see #22.407.

12.1   "Frauenbewegung und Fruchtbarkeit," *Panther*, Berlin 2 (1913/14), 16–23.
12.12   Feminism and Fertility.
12.13   Also reprinted in *Umsturz* under a different title; see #22.405.

13.1   "Versuche einer Philosophie des Lebens," *Die Weissen Blätter*, Leipzig 1 (1913/14), 203–33.
13.12   Attempts towards a Philosophy of Life.
13.13   Reprinted in *Umsturz*; see #22.408.

14.1   "Zur Rehabilitierung der Tugend," *Die Weissen Blätter*, Leipzig 1 (1913/14), 360–78.
14.12   Towards the Rehabilitation of Virtue.
14.13   This article appeared under a pseudonym. Reprinted in *Umsturz*; see #22.401.

15.1   "Der Bourgeois," *Die Weissen Blätter*, Leipzig 1 (1913/14), 581–602.
15.12   The Bourgeois.
15.13   Reprinted in *Umsturz*; see #22.409.

16.1   "Über das Tragische," *Die Weissen Blätter*, Leipzig 1 (1913/14), 758–76.
16.12   On the Tragic.
16.13   Reprinted in *Umsturz*; see #22.403.
16.14   "On the Tragic," translated by Bernard Stambler. *Cross Currents* 4 (Winter, 1954), 178–91.

17.1   "Die Zukunft des Kapitalismus," *Die Weissen Blätter*, Leipzig 1 (1913/14), 933–48.
17.12   The Future of Capitalism.
17.13   Reprinted in *Umsturz*; see #22.409.

18.1   "Der Bourgeois und die religiösen Mächte," *Die Weissen Blätter*, Leipzig 1 (1913/14), 1171–91.
18.12   The Bourgeois and the Forces of Religion.
18.13   Reprinted in *Umsturz*; see #22.409.

19.1   "Ethik. Ein Forschungsbericht," *Jahrbücher der Philosophie*,

Eine kritische Übersicht der Philosophie der Gegenwart. Edited by Max Frischeisen-Köhler. Vol. II. Berlin, 1914, 81–118.

19.12   Ethics. A Research Report.

20.1   "Der Genius des Krieges," *Die Neue Rundschau*, Berlin 25 (1914), 1327–52.

20.12   The Spirit of War.

20.13   Reprinted following year. See #21.1 and # 30.101.

21.1   *Der Genius des Krieges und der deutsche Krieg*. Leipzig: Verlag der Weissen Bücher, 1915. 444 pp.

21.12   The Spirit of War and the German War.

21.2   Second edition: *ibid.*, 1916.

21.3   Third edition: newly revised, *ibid.*, 1917. See # 20.1.

22.1   *Abhandlungen und Aufsätze*. In two volumes. Leipzig: Verlag der Weissen Bücher, 1915. 367 pp. and 411 pp.

22.12   Essays and Articles.

22.2   Second edition under the title: *Vom Umsturz der Werte*. Leipzig: Neue Geist-Verlag. 1919, 313 pp. and 345 pp.

22.22   On the Overthrow of Values.

22.3   Third edition: Leipzig: Reinhold, 1923, 308 pp. and 329 pp.

22.4   The fourth edition appeared as volume three of the *Gesammelte Werke*. M. Scheler, *Vom Umsturz der Werte*. Abhandlungen und Aufsätze. Vierte durchgesehene Auflage. Herausgegeben von Maria Scheler. Bern: Francke, 1955. 450 pp.

22.43   This edition reprints the three Forewords from the first three editions. The work is published as one volume and contains the usual appendices.

22.401   "Zur Rehabilitierung der Tugend," 13–31.

22.4013   See #14.1.

22.402   "Das Ressentiment im Aufbau der Moralen," 33–147.

22.4023   See #7.1 for full bibliographical details.

22.403   "Zum Phänomen des Tragischen," 149–69.

22.4033   See #16.1.

22.404   "Zur Idee des Menschen," 171–95.

22.4042   Towards the Idea of Man.

22.4043   Its first appearance was in the 1915 edition.
22.405   "Zum Sinn der Frauenbewegung," 197–222.
22.4052   Towards the Meaning of Feminism.
22.4053   See #12.1.
22.406   "Die Idole der Selbsterkenntnis," 213–92.
22.4062   The Idols of Self-Knowledge.
22.4063   See #6.1.
22.407   "Die Psychologie der sogenannten Rentenhysterie und der rechte Kampf gegen das Übel," 203–309.
22.4073   See #11.1.
22.408   "Versuche einer Philosophie des Lebens, Nietzsche-Dilthey-Bergson," 311–39.
22.4083   See #13.1.
22.409   "Der Bourgeois—Der Bourgeois und die religiösen Mächte—Die Zukunft des Kapitalismus," 341–95.
22.4093   These three essays appeared in *Die Weissen Blätter* during 1914. See #15.1, #17.1 and #18.1.

23.1   "Das Nationale in der Philosophie Frankreichs," *Der Neue Merkur*, München (1915), 513–30.
23.12   Military Nationalism in the Philosophy of France.
23.13   Reprinted in *Krieg und Aufbau* and in *Soziologie*; see #30.103 and #62.20B2.

24.1   "Europa und der Krieg," *Die Weissen Blätter*, Leipzig 2 (1915), 124–27; 244–49 and 376–80.
24.12   Europe and the War.
24.13   See #29.1 and #30.101.

25.1   "Liebe und Erkenntnis," *Die Weissen Blätter*, Leipzig 2 (1915), 991–1016.
25.12   Love and Knowledge.
25.13   Reprinted both in *Krieg und Aufbau* (see #30.109) and #62.20A5 in *Soziologie*.

26.1   "Über östliches und westliches Christentum," *Die Weissen Blätter*, Leipzig 2 (1915), 1263–81.
26.12   Concerning Eastern and Western Christianity.
26.13   Reprinted both in *Krieg und Aufbau* and in *Soziologie*; see #30.102 and #62.20A6.

27.1	"Zur Psychologie der Nationen," *Die Neue Rundschau*, Berlin 26 (1915), 999–1001.
27.12	The Psychology of Nations.
27.13	Reprinted under different title both in *Krieg und Aufbau* and in *Soziologie*; see #30.104 and #62.20B1.
28.1	"Soziologische Neuorientierung und die Aufgabe der deutschen Katholiken nach dem Krieg," *Hochland*, München 13 (1915/16), Bd. 1, 385–406; 682–700 and Bd. 2, 188–214 and 257–94.
28.12	Sociological Reorientation and the Task of German Catholics after the War.
28.13	Reprinted in *Krieg und Aufbau*; see #30.107.
29.1	"Der Genius des Krieges und das Gesamterlebnis unseres Krieges," *Der Grosse Krieg*, edited by v. E. Jäckh, Gotha: Perthes, 1916, 276–87.
29.12	The Spirit of the War and the Total Experience of Our War.
29.13	See #21.1; reprinted in *Krieg und Aufbau*; see #30.101 and #24.1.
30.1	*Krieg und Aufbau*, Leipzig: Verlag der Weissen Bücher, 1916. 432 pp.
30.12	War and Reconstruction.
30.13	A collection of many published articles; many of these are reprinted in *Soziologie*; see #62.1. There are nine parts to this volume.
30.101	"Der Krieg als Gesamterlebnis."
30.1012	The War as a Collective Experience.
30.1013	See #20.1 and #29.1.
30.102	"Über östliches und westliches Christentum."
30.1023	See #26.1; also reprinted in *Soziologie*; see #62.20A6.
30.103	"Das Nationale im Denken Frankreichs."
30.1033	See #23.1; also reprinted in *Soziologie*; see #62.20B2.
30.104	"Über die Nationalideen der grossen Nationen."
30.1042	On the National Ideas of the Great Nations.
30.1043	See #27.1; also reprinted in *Soziologie*; see #62.20B1.
30.105	"Bemerkungen zum Geiste und den ideellen Grundlagen der Demokratien der grossen Nationen."
30.1052	Remarks on the Spirit and the Ideal Bases of Democracy of the great Nations.

112   BIBLIOGRAPHY

30.1053	Reprinted in *Soziologie*; see #62.20B3
30.106	"Über Gesinnungs- und Zweckmilitarismus. Eine Studie zur Psychologie des Militarismus."
30.1062	On the Disposition and Goals of Militarism. A Study in the Psychology of Militarism.
30.1063	Reprinted in *Soziologie*; see #62.20B4.
30.107	"Soziologische Neuorientierung und die Aufgabe der deutschen Katholiken nach dem Kriege."
30.1072	Sociological Reorientation and the Task of German Catholics after the War.
30.1073	See #28.1.
30.108	"Vom Sinn des Leides."
30.1082	On the Meaning of Suffering
30.1083	See #591.; expanded and reprinted in *Soziologie*; see #62.20A3
30.109	"Liebe und Erkenntnis."
30.1092	Love and Knowledge.
30.1093	This is a reprint; see #25.1. Reprinted again in *Soziologie*; see #62.20A5.

31.1	"Die christliche Gemeinschaftsidee und die gegenwärtige Welt," *Hochland*, München 14 (1916), Bd. 1, 641–72.
31.12	The Christian Idea of Community and the Contemporary World.
31.13	Reprinted in *Ewigen*; see #51.404.

32.1	"Von kommenden Dingen," *Hochland*, München 14 (1916/17), Bd. 2, 385–411.
32.12	Concerning Things to Come.

33.1	"1789 und 1914," *Archiv für Sozialwissenschaften und Sozialpolitik*, Tübingen 42 (1916/17), 586–605.

34.1	*Die Ursachen des Deutschenhasses.* Eine nationalpädagogische Erörterung. Leipzig: Wolff, 1917, 192 pp.
34.12	The Causes of the Hatred of Germany. A Discussion for National Instruction.
34.13	See #44.13
34.2	Second edition: Leipzig: Neue Geist-Verlag. 1919. 158 pp.

35.1	"Zur Apologetik der Reue," *Summa*, Leipzig 1 (1917/18), 53–83.
35.12	Towards the Defense of Repentance.
35.13	Reprinted under a slightly different title in *Ewigen*; see #51.401.
36.1	"Die christliche Persönlichkeit," *Summa*, Leipzig 1 (1917/18), 144–46.
36.12	The Christian Person.
37.1	"Die deutsche Wissenschaft," *Summa*, Leipzig 1 (1917/18), 151–53.
37.12	German Science.
38.1	"Der orientalische Mensch," *Summa*, Leipzig 1 (1917/18), 158–60.
38.12	Oriental Man.
39.1	"Vom Wesen der Philosophie," *Summa*, Leipzig 1 (1917/18), 40–70.
39.12	On the Essence of Philosophy.
39.13	Reprinted in *Ewigen*; see #51.402.
40.1	"Recht, Staat und Gesellschaft," *Hochland*, München 15 (1917/18), 129–41.
40.12	Right, State and Society.
41.1	"Vom kulturellen Wiederaufbau Europas," *Hochland*, München 15 (1917/18), 497–510 und 663–81.
41.12	The Cultural Reconstruction of Europe.
41.13	Revised and expanded in *Ewigen*; see #51.405.
42.1	"Deutschlands Sendung und der katholische Gedanke," Berlin: *Germania*, 1918, 34 pp.
42.12	Germany's Mission and Catholic Thought.
43.1	"Zur religiösen Erneuerung," *Hochland*, München 16 (1918/19), Bd. 1, 5–21.

43.12   Religious Renewal.
43.13   Reprinted in *Ewigen*; see #51.403.

44.1   "Gedanken des Verstehens," *Westdeutsche Wochenschrift*,
         Köln 1 (1919), 97.
44.12   Thoughts towards Understanding.
44.13   Excerpt from *Die Ursachen des Deutschenhasses*; see #34.1.

45.1   "Innere Widersprüche der deutschen Universitäten,"
         Westdeutsche Wochenschrift, Köln 1 (1919), 493–95; 511;
         524–27; 539–41; 561–53.
45.12   Inner Contradictions in German Universities.

46.1   "Politik und Kultur auf dem Boden der neuen Ord-
         nung," *Der Geist der neuen Volksgemeinschaft*, Fischer, Ber-
         lin, (1919), 30–51.
46.12   Politics and Culture at the Base of the New Order.

47.1   "Prophetischer oder marxistischer Sozialismus," *Hoch-
         land*, München 17 (1919/20), Bd. 1, 71–84.
47.12   Prophetic or Marxist Socialism.
47.13   A lecture of 1919; reprinted in *Soziologie*; see #62.20C2.

48.1   "Von zwei deutschen Krankheiten," *Der Leuchter*, Darm-
         stadt 1 (1919), 161–90.
48.12   Two German Diseases.
48.13   Reprinted in *Soziologie*; see #62.20B5.

49.1   "Der Friede unter den Konfessionen," *Hochland*, Mün-
         chen 18 (1920–21), Bd. 1, 140–47 und 464–86.
49.12   Peace among the Denominations.
49.13   A lecture of 1920; reprinted in *Soziologie*; see #62.20C1.

50.1   "Wert und Würde der christlichen Arbeit," *Jahrbuch der
         Deutschen Katholiken*. Augsburg: Haas & Crabherr, (1920/
         21), 75–89.
50.12   The Value and Dignity of Christian Work.
50.13   Reprinted in *Soziologie*; see #62.20C3.

51.1   *Vom Ewigen im Menschen*, Religiöse Erneuerung. First
         edition (in one volume): Leipzig: Neue Geist-Verlag,
         1921. 725 pp.

51.12	On the Eternal in Man. Religious Renewal.
51.2	Second edition (in two half-volumes), with a larger Foreword: Leipzig: Neue Geist-Verlag, 1923. 278 pp. and 447 pp.
51.3	Third edition (popular edition, abridged, in one volume): Berlin: Neue Geist-Verlag, 1933, 725 pp.
51.4	Fourth edition, *Gesammelte Werke*, Bd. 5, Bern: Francke, 1954. 488 pp.
51.44	M. Scheler, *On the Eternal in Man*. Translated by Bernard Noble. London: SCM Press, Ltd., 1960, 1960. 480 pp.
51.443	Contains a Foreword by August Brunner, a Note on the Author by I. M. Bochenski and a translation of all the appendices from Band 5 of the *Gesammelte Werke*. The translation is uniformly good. The contents are as in *Ewigen*, but some of the titles are more loosely translated in the body of the text.
51.401	"Reue und Wiedergeburt," 27–59.
51.4012	Rependance and Rebirth.
51.4013	See #35.1.
51.402	"Vom Wesen der Philosophie und die moralischen Bedingungen des philosophischen Erkennens," 61–99.
51.402	The Essence of Philosophy and the Moral Conditions for Philosophical Knowledge.
51.4023	See #39.1.
51.403	"Probleme der Religion," 101–354.
51.4032	Problems of Religion.
51.4033	The introductory section appeared in *Hochland* in 1918. See #43.1. The rest of study was printed in *Ewigen* for the first time.
51.404	"Die christliche Liebesidee und die gegenwärtige Welt," 355–401.
51.4041	The Christian Idea of Love and the Contemporary World.
51.4043	See #31.1.
51.405	"Vom kulturellen Wiederaufbau Europas," 403–47.
51.4052	The Cultural Reconstruction of Europe.
51.4053	See #41.1.
52.1	"Die positivistische Geschichtsphilosophie und die Aufgaben einer Soziologie der Erkenntnis," *Kölner Vierteljahreshefte für Sozialwissenschaften*, München 1 (1921), 22–31.

52.12   The Positivistic Philosophy of History and the Tasks of a
         Sociology of Knowledge.
52.13   Reprinted and revised in *Soziologie*; see #62.20A2.

53.1   "Zu W. Jerusalems 'Bemerkungen'" *Kölner Vierteljahres-
         hefte für Sozialwissenschaften*, München 1 (1921), 35–39.
53.12   In Response to some Remarks by W. Jerusalem.

54.1   "Universität und Volkshochschule," A contribution to
         the anthology *Zur Soziologie des Volksbildungswesens*, edited
         by Leopold V. Wiese. München: Duncker und Humbolt,
         1921, 153–91.
54.12   University and the People's College.
54.13   This work was volume 1 of the Publications for the Re-
         search Institute for Social Science in Cologne. This es-
         say was reprinted in *Wissensformen*; see #67.401.

55.1   "Die deutsche Philosophie der Gegenwart," in *Deutsches
         Leben der Gegenwart*, edited by P. Witkop. Berlin: Verlag
         der Bücherfreunde, 1922. 127–224.
55.12   German Philosophy Today.

56.1   "Vom Verrat der Freude" in: *Erster Almanach des Volks-
         verbandes der Bücherfreunde*. Berlin: Wegweiser Verlag,
         1922, 70–76.
56.12   On the Betrayal of Joy.
56.13   Reprinted in *Soziologie*; see #62.20A4.

57.1   "Walter Rathenau," in *Walther Rathenau*. Köln: Marcan
         Block, 1922, 1–22.
57.13   Collaborated with Eduard Heimann and Arthur Baum-
         garten in this tribute to the thought of his friend.
         Reprinted in *Soziologie*; see #62.20E1.

58.1   "Weltanschauungslehre, Soziologie und Weltanschau-
         ungssetzung," *Kölner Vierteljahreshefte für Sozialwissenschaf-
         ten*, München 1 (1922), 18–33.
58.12   Sociology and the Theory and the Formation of *Welt-
         anschauung*.
58.13   Reprinted in *Soziologie*; see #62.20A1.

59.1	"Das Problem des Leidens," in *Germania*, Berlin 53 (March 20, 1923).
59.12	The Problem of Suffering.
59.13	Originally a speech given in Berlin on March 18, 1923. Expanded and reprinted in *Soziologie*; see #62.20A3.

60.1	"Jugendbewegung," *Berliner Tageblatt*. Berlin (1923), Nr. 154.
60.12	The Youth Movement.
60.13	Reprinted in Soziologie; see #62.20E3.

61.2	*Wesen und Formen der Sympathie*, 2. vermehrte Auflage der "Sympathiegefühle," Bonn: Cohen, 1923. 306 pp.
61.22	The Essence and Forms of Sympathy. Second, enlarged edition of "The Feeling of Sympathy."
61.23	This, then, is the second edition of the 1913 work on sympathy. See #8.1. This is now accepted as the working edition.
61.3	Third edition, Bonn: Cohen, 1926. 312 pp.
61.4	Fourth edition, Frankfurt: Schulte-Bulmke, 1931. 311 pp.
61.5	Fifth edition, Frankfurt: Schulte-Bulmke, 1948. 302 pp.
61.54	M. Scheler, *The Nature of Sympathy*, Translated from the German by Peter Heath. With a general introduction to Max Scheler's Work by W. Stark. New Haven: Yale University Press, 1954. i–liv; 1–274.
61.543	This is a translation of the fifth edition: a rather free translation, but faithful to the meaning. This work includes Scheler's prefaces to the first, second and third editions, as well as Maria Scheler's Introductory Note to the fifth edition. Index of topics and of names.

62.1	*Schriften zur Soziologie und Weltanschauungslehre*. Leipzig: Der Neue Geist Verlag, 1923–24.
62.12	Contributions to Sociology and the Theory of *Weltanschauung*.
62.13	This work appeared in four separate parts, under three titles; Volume 1 "Moralia"; 175 pp.; Volume 2 "Nation und Weltanschauung" 174 pp.; Volume 3 "Christentum und Gesellschaft," part 1, 233 pp.; part 2, 173 pp.
62.2	The second edition appeared as volume six of the *Gesam-*

melte Werke. M. Scheler, *Schriften zur Soziologie und Welt-anschauungslehre.* Zweite,durchgesehene Auflage. Mit Zu-sätzen und kleineren Veröffentlichungen aus der Zeit der "Schriften" herausgegeben mit einem Anhang von Maria Scheler. Bern: Francke, 1963. 455 pp.

62.23   This is a compilation of many previously published articles (especially those during the war) and a few new articles. Letters A, B, C, D refer to the four parts of *Soziologie.*

62.20A1   "Weltanschauungslehre, Soziologie und Weltanschau-ungssetzung," 13–26.

62.20A12   Sociology and the Theory and the Plane of *Weltan-schauung.*

62.20A3   See #58.1.

62.20A2   "Über die positivistische Geschichtsphilosophie des Wis-sens," 27–35.

62.20A22   Concerning the Historical Philosophy of Knowledge of the Positivists.

62.20A23   See #51.1.

62.20A3   "Vom Sinn des Leides," 36–72.

62.20A32   On the Meaning of Suffering.

62.20A33   See #30.108 and #59.1.

62.20A4   "Vom Verrat der Freude," 73–76.

62.20A42   On the Betrayal of Joy.

62.20A43   See #56.1.

62.20A5   "Liebe und Erkenntnis," 77–98.

62.20A52   Love and Knowledge.

62.20A53   See #25.1 and #30.109.

62.20A6   "Über östliches und westliches Christentum," 99–114.

62.20A62   Concerning Eastern and Western Christianity.

62.20A63   See #26.1 and #130.102.

62.20B1   "Über die Nationalidee der grossen Nationen," 121–130.

62.20B12   On the National Ideas of the Great Nations.

62.20B13   See #27.1 and #30.104.

62.20B2   "Das Nationale im Denken Frankreichs," 131–157.

62.20B22   Military Nationalism in the Thinking of France.

62.20B23   See #23.1 and #30.103.

62.20B3   "Der Geist und die ideellen Grundlagen der Demokratien der grossen Nationen," 158–186.

62.20B32	The Spirit and the Ideal bases of Democracy of the Great Nations.
62.20B33	See #30.1053.
62.20B4	"Über Gesinnings- und Zweckmilitarismus. Eine Studie zur Psychologie des Militarismus," 187–203.
62.20B42	On the Dispositions and Goals of Militarism. A Study in the Psychology of Militarism.
62.20B43	See #30.106.
62.20B5	"Von zwei deutschen Krankheiten," 204–219.
62.20B52	Two German Diseases.
62.20B53	See #48.1.
62.20C1	"Der Friede unter den Konfessionen," 228–258.
62.20C12	Peace Among the Denominations.
62.20C13	See #49.1.
62.20C2	"Prophetischer oder marxistischer Sozialismus?," 259–272.
62.20C22	Prophetic or Marxist Socialism?
62.20C23	See #47.1.
62.20C3	"Arbeit und Weltanschauung," 273–289.
62.20C32	Work and *Weltanschauung*.
62.20C33	Reprinted with a different title; see #50.1 and #3.1.
62.20C4	"Bevölkerungsprobleme als Weltanschauungsfragen," 290–324.
62.20C42	Population Problems as Questions of *Weltanschauung*.
62.20C43	From a Congress on social Questions held at Cologne in 1921.
62.20D	Zusätze, 325–358. Short supplementary pieces.
62.20E	Short publications from the time of *Soziologie*.
62.20E1	"Walther Rathenau: Eine Würdigung zu seinem Gedächtnis," 359–376.
62.20E12	Walter Rathenau: A Tribute to His Memory.
62.20E13	See #57.1.
62.20E2	"Ernst Troeltsch als Soziologe," 377–90.
62.20E22	Ernst Troeltsch as a Sociologist.
62.20E23	See #63.1.
62.20E3	"Jugendbewegung," 391–96.
62.20E32	The Youth Movement.
62.20E33	See #60.1.
63.1	"Ernst Troeltsch als Soziologe," *Kölner Vierteljahreshefte für Soziologie*, Leipzig 3 (1923–24), 7–21.

63.12   Ernst Troeltsch as Sociologist.
63.13   Reprinted in *Soziologie*; see #62.20E2.

64.1   "Probleme einer Soziologie des Wissens," in: *Versuche zu einer Soziologie des Wissens*: edited by Max Scheler. München: Duncker & Humblot, 1924. 1–146 pp.
64.12   Problems for a Sociology of Knowledge.
64.13   Amplified and reprinted in 1926 in *Wissensformen*; see #67.201.

65.1   "Wissenschaft und soziale Struktur," in: *Verhandlungen des Vierten Deutschen Soziologentages am 29. und 30. September 1924 in Heidelberg*. Tübingen: Mohr (1925), 118–80.
65.12   Science and social Structure.

66.1   *Die Formen des Wissens und die Bildung*. Bonn: Cohen, 1925. 48 pp.
66.12   Forms of Knowledge and Culture.
66.13   Reprinted in *Weltanschauung*; see #74.202.

67.1   *Die Wissensformen und die Gesellschaft*. Leipzig: Neue Geist-Verlag, 1926. 567 pp.
67.12   Forms of Knowledge and Society.
67.2   Second edition appeared as volume eight of the *Gesammelte Werke*. M. Scheler, *Die Wissensformen und die Gesellschaft*. Zweite, durchgesehene Auflage. Mit Zusätzen. Herausgegeben von Maria Scheler. Bern: Francke, 1960. 536 pp.
67.201   "Probleme einer Soziologie des Wissens," 15–190.
67.2012   Problems of a Sociology of Knowledge.
67.2013   This is an expanded reprint of #64.1.
67.202   "Erkenntnis und Arbeit. Eine Studie über Wert und Grenzen des pragmatischen Princips in der Erkenntnis der Welt," 191–382.
67.2022   Knowledge and Work. A Study concerning Value and the Limitations of the Pragmatic Principle in the Knowledge of Value.
67.2023   This particular study on work appeared here in *Wissensformen* for the first time.
67.203   "Universität und Volkshochschule," 383–420.

67.2032 The University and the People's College.
67.2033 A reprint from 1921; see #54.1.
67.204 "Zusätze aus den nachgelassenen Manuskripten," 421–69.
67.2042 Supplements from remaining Manuscripts.

68.1 "Mensch und Geschichte," *Die Neue Rundschau*, Berlin 37 (1926), 449–76.
68.12 Man and History
68.13 Reprinted in *Weltanschauung*; see #74.204.

69.1 "Spinoza. Zum 250. Todestage des Philosophen," *Kölner Zeitung*, Köln (1927), Literatur- und Unterhaltungsblatt. Beilage Nr. 134 & 138.
69.12 Spinoza. In Memory of the 250th year of the Philosopher's Death.
69.13 Reprinted in *Weltanschauung*; see #74.203.

70.1 "Die Sonderstellung des Menschen," *Der Leuchter*, Darmstadt 8 (1927). 161–254.
70.12 Man's Special Place.
70.13 A separate special edition appeared under the title *Die Stellung des Menschen im Kosmos*. Darmstadt; Reichl, 1928. 115 pp. (The Place of Man in the Cosmos).
70.2 Second edition, 1929, *ibid*.
70.3 Third edition, 1930, *ibid*.
70.4 Fourth edition, München: Nymphenburger Verlagsanstalt, 1947. 99 pp.
70.5 Fifth edition, 1949, *ibid*.
70.6 Sixth edition, Bern: Francke, 1962. 99 pp.
70.64 M. Scheler, *Man's Place in Nature*. Translated with an Introduction by Hans Meyerhoff. Boston: Beacon Press, 1961. 105 pp.
70.643 The translator has edited the work, changed notes, added headings and was very free with the text itself. Exact reimpression of this work was made in paperback by The Noonday Press, 1962.

71.1 "Idealismus-Realismus." *Philosophischer Anzeiger*. 2. Bonn: Cohen, 1927.
71.12 Idealism-Realism.

72.1   "Philosophische Weltanschauung. *Münchner Neueste Nach-*
            richten. München (1928), vom 5. Mai.
72.12   Philosophical *Weltanschauung.*
72.13   Reprinted in *Weltanschauung*; see #74.201.

After Scheler's death, the following works were published from among
his writings finished at that time.

73.1   "Der Mensch im Weltalter des Ausgleichs," in: *Ausgleich*
            als Schicksal und Aufgabe, Berlin: Rothschild, (1929), 31–63.
73.12   Man in the Era of Adjustment.
73.13   Reprinted in *Weltanschauung*; see #74.205.

74.1   *Philosophische Weltanschauung.* Bonn: Cohen, 1929. 185 pp.
74.12   Philosophical *Weltanschauung.*
74.2   Second paperback edition. Bern: Francke, 1954. 135 pp.
74.24   M. Scheler, *Philosophical Perspectives.* Translated from the
            German by Oscar A. Haac. Boston: Beacon Press, 1958.
            144 pp.
74.243   The translation of the title itself (and the first essay
            "Philosopher's Outlook") is highly misleading. This is a
            fair literary translation, but very inadequate for technical
            and philosophical phrases.
74.201   "Philosophische Weltanschauung."
74.2012   Philosophical *Weltanschauung.*
74.2013   See #72.1.
74.202   "Die Formen des Wissens und die Bildung."
74.2022   Forms of Knowledge and Culture.
74.2023   See #66.1.
74.203   "Spinoza. Eine Rede."
74.2032   Spinoza. An Address.
74.2033   See #69.1.
74.204   "Mensch und Geschichte."
74.2042   Man and History.
74.2043   See #68.1.
74.205   "Der Mensch im Weltalter des Ausgleiches."
74.2052   Man in the Era of Adjustment.
74.2053   See #73.1.

From Scheler's early unpublished manuscripts there were published posthumously the following works.

75.1   *Die Idee des Friedens und der Pazifismus,* Berlin: Neue Geist-Verlag, 1931, 63 pp.

75.12   The Idea of Peace and Pacifism.

75.13   A lecture delivered in 1927.

76.1   *Schriften aus dem Nachlass, Bd. 1 Zur Ethik und Erkenntnislehre.* Edited by Maria Scheler, Berlin: Neue Geist-Verlag, 1933. 468 pp.

76.2   Second enlarged edition of this work is Volume Ten of the *Gesammelte Werke.* M. Scheler, *Schriften aus dem Nachlass.* Band I Zur Ethik und Erkenntnislehre. Zweite, durchgesehene und erweiterte Auflage. Mit einem Anhang herausgegeben von Maria Scheler. Bern: Francke, 1957. 583 pp.

76.22   Posthumous Writings. Volume I. Towards Ethics and Epistemology.

76.23   Collection of writings from 1911 to 1914.

76.201   "Tod und Fortleben," 9–64.

76.2012   Death and Life Hereafter.

76.2013   From manuscripts dating back to 1913–14.

76.202   "Über Scham and Schamgefühl," 65–154.

76.2022   Concerning Shame and the Feeling of Shame.

76.2023   From 1913; see #10.1.

76.203   "Zur Phänomenologie und Metaphysik der Freiheit," 155–77.

76.2032   Towards the Phenomenology and the Metaphysics of Freedom.

76.2033   From 1912–14.

76.204   "Absolutsphäre und Realsetzung der Gottesidee," 179–253.

76.2042   The Absolute Sphere and the Real Place of the Idea of God.

76.2043   From 1915–16.

76.205   "Vorbilder und Führer," 255–343.

76.2052   Models and Leaders.

76.2053   From 1911–14.

76.206   "Ordo Amoris," 345–76.

76.2062   The Order of Love.
76.2063   From 1916.
76.207   "Phänomenologie und Erkenntnistheorie," 377–429.
76.2072   Phenomenology and Epistemology.
76.2073   From 1913–14.
76.208   "Lehre von drei Tatsachen," 431–502.
76.2082   Theory of the Three Facts.
76.2083   From 1911–12.

Since 1933 a number of reprints and excerpts from previously published articles have appeared. These items are omitted here.

INDEX

absolute 14, 12–13, 32, 33, 92
act (spiritual act) 17, 25, 28–29, 36, 52, 53, 60, 90, 91; see *Akt*
adjustment 82, 82n4
aesthetics 4, 42; aesthetic values 97
affection, affective phenomena 2, 90; see emotions
Akt (act q.v.) 17, 25
alien *I* 30, 50–53, 55, 57–59; see Thou
analogy, argument of 40–41, 54, 57, 58, 59
angels 18, 29n2, 93, 99
Anschauung (intuition q.v.) 3–4
anthropology 7, 14, 16, 19, 31, 62, 63–64, 101; philosophical 7, 19, 31
a priori 11, 32, 56, 68, 76, 79, 95
Arbeitswelt (world of everyday experience) 3
Aristotle 14, 20, 93
arithmetic 3n1
asceticism 12, 23, 31, 33n3
atheism 19
atomic energy 20
attitude 11; natural 12–13, 14; philosophical 12–13; scientific 12–13; see *Weltanschauung*
Aufschwung (upsurge) 12, 23
Augustine 2

Becker, H. 78n4
being 2, 12–13, 15, 16, 17–18, 19, 20; being and man 31–37; see metaphysics
benevolence 80–81, 88–89
Bergson, H. 12, 39, 46
Bernard, St. 103
biology 16, 17n4, 19, 22, 23n1
body 28, 29, 30, 47, 73; knowing the body of the other 39–41, 59; body-*I* 60, 90, 99; see environment, *I*
bracketing 13, 17, 40n2; see suspension
Buddha 12, 46

Cairns, D. 60

capitalism 2
Cassirer, E. 36n3
"Catholic Period" 647, 8n, 96, 102–03
Catholicism 6, 7, 8n, 33
cause, causal explanation 9, 40–41, 40n2; connections 9n2; unity in man 47, 47n2
Christ 92, 96
Christian 19, 46, 81, 89, 91, 94, 96, 102
civilization 63–63, 82n5
Collins, J. 5n3, 8n, 13n1, 13n3
community 27, 51, 53, 56, 57, 61, 66; phenomenology of 1, 37, 102–03; life-community 69, 72, 87–88, 98; person-community 69–70, 72, 76, 81, 88, 93–96, 98
"community of feeling" (*Mit-einander-fühlen*) 77
Comte, A. 62n, 64–65, 74
Conrad, T. 4
Crusoe, Robinson 56, 68, 93
culture 3, 82n2; cultural forms 1; see civilization

D'Arcy, M. 92n1
Darwin, C. 39, 43
Dasein (contingent being) 31, 34, 35, 44, 48, 48n, 65
data (*Sachverhalte*) 11, 17
Daubert, J. 4, 4n2
death 5
Defoe, D. 56
deity 7, 36
Dewey, J. 21, 22n1
Dilthey, W. 1, 74
Dionysius 19, 37
doxa (opinion) 12
Drang, Gefühlsdrang, Urdrang, Lebensdrang (basic drive) 20, 33, 35, 64, 97, 99
drive see *Drang*
Dupuy, M. 2, 2n1, 2n2, 4n1, 4n3, 7n1, 7n2, 85n1
Durkheim, E. 62n
"ecstatic" 21, 23